CANADA AND MISSIONS FOR PEACE

CONTRIBUTORS

Lloyd Axworthy
Minister of Foreign Affairs, Canada

Kenneth D. Bush
International Development Research Centre, Ottawa, Canada

Gérard Hervouët
Department of Political Science, Université Laval, Sainte-Foy, Canada

Robert Miller
Parliamentary Centre, Ottawa, Canada

Andrés Pérez
Department of Political Science, The University of Western Ontario, London, Canada

Necla Tschirgi
International Development Research Centre, Ottawa, Canada

Gregory Wirick
Parliamentary Centre, Ottawa, Canada

CANADA AND MISSIONS FOR PEACE

Lessons from NICARAGUA, CAMBODIA, and SOMALIA

Edited by

Gregory Wirick
and Robert Miller

INTERNATIONAL DEVELOPMENT RESEARCH CENTRE
Ottawa • Cairo • Dakar • Johannesburg • Montevideo • Nairobi • New Delhi • Singapore

Published by the International Development Research Centre
PO Box 8500, Ottawa, ON, Canada K1G 3H9

Canadian Cataloguing in Publication Data

Main entry under title :
Canada and missions for peace : lessons from Nicaragua, Cambodia, and Somalia

Issued also in French under title : Les missions de paix et le Canada.

Includes bibliographical references.

ISBN 0-88936-867-8

1. Economic assistance, Canadian — Political aspects — Developing countries.
2. Economic assistance, Canadian — Nicaragua.
3. Economic assistance, Canadian — Cambodia.
4. Economic assistance, Canadian — Somalia.
5. Canada — Foreign relations — 1945– .
6. Security, International.
7. Peace.
I. Wirick, Gregory.
II. Miller, Robert, 1941– .
III. International Development Research Centre (Canada).

HC59.72C32 1998 338.91'710124 C98-980300-7

IDRC Books endeavours to produce environmentally friendly publications. All paper used is recycled as well as recyclable. All inks and coatings are vegetable-based products.

To the memory of
Gregory Wirick (1952–1998),
a valued friend, colleague, and
leader in the new field
of peacebuilding.

— RM

Contents

FOREWORD

The requirements of peace preservation in the future may not always be satisfied by skilful improvisation and by the willingness of a few to do their duty. The growing interest in improving peace-keeping methods must be broadly stimulated into advance planning and preparation. Canada, I know, is resolved to draw on its own experience in a way which will give leadership and encouragement in this effort.

— Lester B. Pearson
(Dag Hammarskjold Memorial Lecture, 1964)

One of the defining features of Canada's role in the world, both for Canadians and the international community, has been our unflagging support for United Nations peacekeeping. Up until the beginning of this decade, when the number of intrastate conflicts literally exploded, we boasted a perfect record, having participated in all UN-sponsored peacekeeping missions.

That was a far simpler world. Actors were clearly identified, the missions were simple, and the rules understood. The reality we faced in the aftermath of the Cold War was radically different. Not only was the United Nations overwhelmed by the demands put on it by the multiplication of conflicts, but it had to face a completely different type of situation — one for which it was ill-equipped. The UN Secretary General's *An Agenda for Peace,* its supplement (Boutros-Ghali 1992, 1995), and the Canadian report entitled *Towards a Rapid Reaction Capability for the United Nations* (GOC 1995b) were among the first attempts to come to grips with a new breed of threat to international security — a threat coming from within states rather than between them. These reports also reflected a growing international preoccupation with human vulnerability and well-being — so-called human security.

The strain caused by the proliferation of intrastate conflict was also acutely felt by the traditional contributors of troops, like Canada. Although Canadians remain attached to our role as peacekeepers, it is not always easy to comprehend fully the new situation faced by Canadian soldiers, diplomats, and nongovernmental representatives in the field. Case studies such as those presented in this book serve not only to broaden our understanding of the management of contemporary conflict. They also bring about a better appreciation of the difficulties and complexities facing Canada in its attempts to fulfil its traditional role in this new environment.

Nicaragua, Cambodia, and Somalia are perfect examples of the challenges now confronting global efforts to build lasting peace in countries and regions experiencing armed conflict. They also clearly demonstrate the diverse range of actions that the UN Security Council has been called upon to undertake in response to this new type of conflict. Originally charged to monitor truces between warring parties, peacekeeping operations changed radically in the late 1980s, when they were obliged to transform themselves into comprehensive peace-support operations including humanitarian and civilian police operations, as well as efforts in national reconciliation and reconstruction.

More than being a simple improvement in peacekeeping methods, an actual mutation in the approach to, and management of, operations has been forced upon the international community. These new conflicts are often deeply rooted in religious, ethnic, and cultural differences and are often unleashed by the weakness or failure of states. To prevent, to manage, and to resolve such conflicts, and — further — to establish a self-sustaining peace, requires a comprehensive and integrated approach. Peacekeeping is no longer a stand-alone function but rather an equal and vital partner (along with preventive action, peacemaking, and peacebuilding) in what are called peace-support operations, whose aims are not only to maintain peace but also to create an environment suitable for the establishment of a lasting peace.

Again, the three cases in this book demonstrate concretely the range of intervention and the level of effort required from the contributing states. Achieving and monitoring a cease-fire is only the beginning. Rebuilding state institutions, re-establishing civilian authority and the rule of law, organizing free and fair elections, and lifting landmines from the ground are only a few of the tasks involved in supporting and building peace. Moreover, as pointed out in this book, such an approach demands close cooperation between all the organizations involved: military peacekeepers, UN specialized agencies, nongovernmental orgainzations, churches, and so forth. As demonstrated by the cases selected herein, there is no fixed, definitive model nor sequence of intervention applicable to all situations; however, a clear understanding of the task at hand is emerging.

As we have seen recently with the mandate for the mission to be deployed in Sierra Leone, the scope of the equation for security has been greatly broadened. It now ranges from the creation and maintenance of a secure environment to the demobilization, disarmament, and reintegration of former combatants; from the reconstruction of civil institutions such as the judiciary to long-term capacity building; from military and police training to deployment of human rights observers. Each one of these "parts of the equation" has a military, civilian, police, and humanitarian dimension of varying size, and they are all interdependent.

Another disturbing aspect of this kind of conflict, for which we are still ill-equipped, is the fact that the huge majority of casualties (as high as 90%) are civilians. As well, they are most often from the most vulnerable segment of the population: women and children. Unfortunately, existing international law regulating interstate war affords little protection to individuals caught up in a "civil" war. It has now become clear that the existing regime of humanitarian law needs to evolve to redress this situation. In this context, the Ottawa Convention banning the use of landmines and the recent creation of the International Criminal Court are breaking new ground. Controlling the proliferation of small arms and prohibiting the use of child soldiers would also contribute to mitigating some of the most destructive effects of intrastate armed conflict.

I can only commend and welcome the intellectual effort undertaken by the authors in bringing to the fore this important humanitarian agenda. By doing so, they make a valuable contribution to our understanding of such conflicts. Moreover, I believe this book will also reaffirm for Canadians their traditional commitment to helping those victimized by conflict.

More than ever, and as foreseen by Lester Pearson, the requirements for peace preservation in the post-Cold War environment cannot be satisfied only with "skilful improvisation and by the willingness of a few to do their duty." It requires the efforts of all of us, as we retool ourselves to respond to the evolving challenges of conflict and human security.

Lloyd Axworthy
Minister of Foreign Affairs, Canada
29 September 1998

PREFACE

Canada and Missions for Peace resulted from a convergence of several strands of academic research, policy development, and institutional collaboration around the new peacebuilding agenda. This book is also an expression of a new approach to international affairs that explores the complex interface between foreign policy, international security, and international development.

Canada and Missions for Peace, originally conceived as a follow-up to an earlier book edited by Robert Miller, *Aid as Peacemaker: Canadian Development Assistance and Third World Conflict*, was intended to be an examination of Canada's engagement in international efforts to bring peace to three countries caught in the ravages of violent conflict: Nicaragua, Cambodia, and Somalia. However, the book's evolution coincided with, and was influenced by, a critical assessment within Canada and the international community of the new peacebuilding agenda.

Peacebuilding is a fairly new concept and an even newer field of study. It has been only in the last 2 years, for example, that Canada established peacebuilding programs or units in the Department of Foreign Affairs and International Trade, the Canadian International Development Agency, and the International Development Research Centre (IDRC). During the same period, a number of nongovernmental organizations (NGOs) and academic programs with a special focus on the practice or study of peacebuilding also emerged. Yet, only a decade ago, peacebuilding was a concept barely used within either research or policy circles. Moreover, NGOs that practiced peacebuilding rarely identified their work in those terms.

Students of international affairs agree that it was the dismantling of the Berlin Wall — a symbol of a dangerously divided world — that gave the international community the opportunity to view peace not simply as the preservation of the precarious balance of power among competing blocs, but as an ongoing concern for human security in a rapidly changing global system. But it was former United Nations (UN) Secretary-General Boutros Boutros-Ghali who gave political currency to the concept of peacebuilding when he submitted his report *An Agenda for Peace* to the 47th Session of the UN on 17 June 1992.

The expectations and hopes for a new world order that accompanied the fall of the Berlin Wall and underlaid the Secretary-General's report were quickly put to the test with the violent thrust of local and regional conflicts into the international arena in the early 1990s. The international community responded to these crises with a variety of instruments and varying degrees of success. The elaborate architecture of international security that had evolved since 1945 and rested on state-centric concepts of security in a system of sovereign states proved inadequate for dealing with the violent threats to peace and security that emerged after the Cold War. The result has been a much-needed, critical rethinking among scholars, as well as among policymakers, of the nature and dynamics of peace and conflict in the final years of the

20th century. It is still too early to tell whether such rethinking will ultimately lead to the construction of a new peacebuilding architecture that combines a concern for international security at the systemic level with a concern for human security at the societal level.

Canada and Missions for Peace is part of a growing wave of research and scholarship critically examining the imperatives of peacebuilding in the post-Cold War era. However, in several ways, this book takes a unique approach. First and foremost, it focuses on the motivations, dynamics, and impacts of Canada's involvement in international peacebuilding efforts. Second, going beyond conventional analyses of Canadian foreign policy, it situates Canada's peacebuilding efforts in the complex domestic and international conditions that obtained in three very different contexts: Nicaragua, Cambodia, and Somalia. Finally, drawing on Canada's early experiences with peacebuilding, it provides sobering insights and useful recommendations to guide future policy and programing in peacebuilding.

Although this special collection focuses primarily on Canada's engagement in three distinct international missions for peace, it sheds light on the multiple interests and policy imperatives that underlie all peacebuilding efforts at local, national, and international levels. Thus, it is intended to make a contribution to the broader international discourse on peacebuilding.

Canada and Missions for Peace also represents a new form of collaboration among academics and policy-research institutes. Drawing on the work of researchers from three different Canadian academic institutions, the project was made possible through a productive partnership between IDRC and the Parliamentary Centre — two institutions that recently expanded their programs to address the challenges faced by countries undergoing political transition after violent conflict.

This volume is a contribution to the programing objectives of IDRC's new Peacebuilding and Reconstruction Program Initiative, which supports research on concrete experiences in peacebuilding and reconstruction in order to generate a knowledge base to guide policy and action at the local, national, and international levels. In many ways, the Parliamentary Centre is a natural ally in this task, as it was one of the first Canadian actors to begin wrestling with the conceptual and practical challenge of fitting together the political, economic, and social pieces of the peacebuilding puzzle. The type of research contained in *Canada and Missions for Peace* can play a catalytic role in facilitating dialogue, consensus building, coalition building, and policy development in both the North and the South.

The approach adopted in this volume also supports the multilevel programing framework of the Peacebuilding and Reconstruction Program Initiative. Through its detailed case studies, *Canada and Missions for Peace* generates country-specific insights and understanding. Yet, its broader examination of the idea of a mission for peace pushes us to consider the larger, generalizable features of these cases that could inform future decisions by development actors in conflict-prone regions. The book's twofold focus on the specific experiences of the cases and the broader set of operational and policy issues they raise presents a well-grounded and analytical argument that, it is hoped, will be a useful contribution to ongoing discussion of the challenge of peacebuilding and postconflict reconstruction.

Robert Miller
Parliamentary Centre
Ottawa, Canada

Necla Tschirgi
International Development Research Centre
Ottawa, Canada

Chapter 1

INTRODUCTION

CONFLICT IN AN ERA OF RADICAL CHANGE

Gregory Wirick and Robert Miller

Canada is in search of new roles and a new policy framework in the transition period known, for now, as the post-Cold War era. This period is less than a decade old, but it has been tumultuous for many key foreign-policy actors. With the pace of change being so rapid, the media and the many new voices now engaged in international affairs being so impatient, and the pursuit of interests being so perilous, some weary policymakers might be tempted to identify this period as a far more confusing time for Canadian diplomacy than any during the 40 years of the Cold War.

This volume deals with selected aspects of Canada's engagement with the new international environment. Specifically, it examines Canada's involvement in the resolution of prolonged deadly conflicts in Nicaragua, Cambodia, and Somalia. We refer to these international operations under the United Nations (UN) umbrella as *missions for peace.* The study focuses primarily on Canada's role in these missions in light of Canadian security interests. However, in keeping with international trends, security is defined broadly to include issues pertaining to economic and social development. By examining several of Canada's foreign-policy missions in the post-Cold War era, the book seeks to lay out potential guidelines for future decision-making.

By way of introduction to these themes, it is important to acknowledge the radical nature of the current era. The chief developments of the new era are manifold:

- The stunning collapse of the Soviet bloc and the worldwide disillusionment with the Marxist–Leninist doctrine that had exerted such a powerful influence in much of the Third World during the Cold War;
- The emergence of the United States as the sole superpower, albeit a Lilliputian one constrained by many strings;
- The spread of capitalism around the world, accompanied by the emergence of global economic competition as the new leitmotif of international relations;
- The concomitant decline of the sovereignty of nation-states;
- The proliferation of international actors and policy issues on the global stage; and
- The increasing appeal of nationalist or even racialist solutions to the problems of order and authority in many parts of the world, accompanied by a new and devastating trade in arms.

The effects throughout the world of two of these developments — the end of Soviet power and the rise of globalism and economic competition — can only be described as revolutionary.

It is true that the Cold War era had its own insecurities and anxieties; nevertheless, the relative order and clarity of the Cold War system — with its hierarchies of power and its well- established ways of doing things — have given way to a less stable and less secure environment that is fluid, complicated by multipolarity, and confused by the multiplicity of actors. For many of the foreign-policy elite, the new system seems systemless and is a sobering reminder of a lost discipline. Others consider the end of the Cold War a welcome relief: it brought an overdue liberation of millions of oppressed peoples; an end to the perversities of superpower competition and the arms race; and prospects for greater consensus within the UN Security Council.

It turns out that both the optimists and the pessimists are correct. The immense Soviet empire has receded, the arms competition between the superpowers has ceased, and agreements to reduce arms stocks are gradually being implemented. However, vacuums of power dot the world, the lingering aftereffects of the Cold War and the withdrawal of superpower influence and interest. As societies and states adjust to new power realities, conflicts within states abound. Indeed, the sources of conflict and violence during the post-Cold War era have been primarily within states. This is exemplified by the breakdown or weakening of many nation-states with the emergence of identity groups, each with its own brand of exclusiveness. Regarding the nature of this conflict, Ignatieff (1997, p. 59) wrote the following:

> *Of the nearly fifty conflicts today, few conform to the classic pattern of professional war between states. They include armed insurrections and guerrilla campaigns against unpopular regimes, ethnic-minority uprisings against majority rule, and jackal gangs roaming freely amid failed states.*

Accompanied by breakdowns in civil authority, vast refugee movements and displacements of peoples within their own borders, and the rise of ethnic and religious fanaticism, these phenomena have created serious regional instabilities in various parts of the world.

In part, the end of the Cold War served to reinforce trends with deep historical roots. Since World War II the number of states has proliferated enormously as the British and other European empires gradually contracted. Fully two-thirds of the contemporary roster of states has been established since 1945. At the beginning of the period, the world had barely 60 states. Through decolonization, that number increased to almost 160 by the end of the Cold War in 1988. More recently, with the breakup of Yugoslavia and the Soviet Union, that number has risen to 180 and is still climbing.

Unfortunately, the legacy of the colonial period has been bitter divisions. The borders for most of Africa's roughly 50 states, for example, were drawn up by the great powers at the Berlin Conference in

1884, with little concern for the ethnic, linguistic, or cultural affinities of Africans. The borders of most of the modern Middle East were drawn equally artificially, deriving from the division of spoils between the French and British after the Ottoman Empire crumbled during World War I. Likewise, the borders of the newly independent former Soviet republics are tentative and tenuous, especially as so many ethnic Russians now live in "the near abroad," beyond Russia's frontiers, a situation that is a persistent source of tension.

Gurr (1994), in a recent study based on an extensive worldwide survey of "minorities at risk," found that "the increase in serious ethnopolitical conflict since the late 1980s is a continuation of a trend that first became evident in the 1960s. The deconstruction of the Soviet bloc nudged the trend upward but did not create it" (Gurr pp. 2–3). Gurr also noted that "the principal issue of the most intense new conflicts is contention for state power among communal groups in Third-World societies." Moreover,

> *Power transitions within states have been the principal, immediate condition of civil and communal warfare, past and present. Two kinds of power transitions have increased in the aftermath of the Cold War: 20 new or redesigned states have come into existence; and a number of states are experimenting with new democratic institutions.*

In many cases, nationalism is providing a new ideology and the new framework that undergirds the exercise of power (Berlin 1992, p. 251):

> *The rise of nationalism is today a world-wide phenomenon, probably the strongest single factor in the newly established states, and in some cases among the minority populations of the older nations. … It might be said that this is an automatic psychological accompaniment of liberation from foreign rule — a natural reaction … against oppression or humiliation of a society that possesses national characteristics.*

The trouble is that this 19th-century doctrine has been a persistent source of strife (Kedourie 1966, p. 115):

> *Nationalism enormously complicates the relations of different groups in mixed areas. Since it advocates a recasting of frontiers and a redistribution of political power to conform with the demands of a particular nationality, it tends to disrupt whatever equilibrium may have been reached between different groups, to reopen settled questions and to renew strife. … Far from increasing political stability and political liberty, nationalism in mixed areas makes for tension and mutual hatred.*

The revival of nationalism is not the only important source of discord in the contemporary world. Hoffman (1995, p. 167) wrote that

> *There is another enemy in today's world: not the violence that results from the clash of mighty powers or from the imposition of the power of the strong on the weak, but the violence that results from chaos from below. The world today is threatened by the disintegration of power — by anomie, which denotes the absence of norms but can also refer to the collision of norms.*

In addition, the increasing incidence of irregular forces, always renowned for their savagery but made more vicious by the devastating effects of modern weaponry, has brought new terrors to these conflicts (Hoffman 1995, p. 61):

> *In the nineteen-nineties, most of the fighting is done by irregulars — the casualties of collapsing societies — or by paramilitary gangs that combine banditry with soldiery. As war passes out of the hands of the state into those of warlords, the rituals of restraint associated with the profession of arms also disintegrate.*

The International Response: An Agenda for Peace

The new intrastate conflicts have spawned many requests for international assistance. Both the UN and the nongovernmental-organization (NGO) community have tried their hands at filling these vacuums of power. The results have been mixed but generally disappointing.

Initially, the international community was very enthusiastic about the use of UN peacekeeping to ensure the delivery of humanitarian aid and to restore order. However, confusion over mandates and rules of engagement resulted in a number of exceedingly treacherous situations — Bosnia, Rwanda, and Somalia are examples. In such cases, combatants are diffuse and difficult to identify; a politically and militarily enforceable cease-fire is often lacking; the central government is weak or nonexistent; and famine, disease, and population displacement are endemic. Such anarchic conditions of recent conflicts have compelled the international community to become deeply involved in the internal affairs of nominally sovereign states.

Some of these missions for peace have been obliged to function in a state-substitution mode, maintaining surveillance over extensive land areas and multiple factions. They have had enhanced requirements, involving an array of military and nonmilitary institutions, because they are complex and multifaceted and because, at times, their objectives have been those of nation-building. In Cambodia, El Salvador, Mozambique, and Namibia, the aim was to provide the basis for the creation or re-creation of national institutions capable of running a modern-day state. Boutros-Ghali (1995, para. 21) detailed the new requirements:

> *The United Nations found itself asked to undertake an unprecedented variety of functions: the supervision of cease-fires; the regroupment and demobilization of forces; their reintegration into civilian life and the destruction of their weapons; the design and implementation of de-mining programmes; the return of refugees and displaced persons; the provision of humanitarian assistance; the supervision of existing administrative structures; the establishment of new police forces; the verification of respect for human rights; the design and supervision of constitutional, judicial and electoral reforms; the observation, supervision and even organization and conduct of elections; and the co-ordination of support for economic rehabilitation and reconstruction.*

These interventions worked reasonably well because there was an international consensus on what should and could be done. In Rwanda and Somalia, however, intervention came in the aftermath of a complete collapse of central authority but without any clear international consensus on what should be done. It is no surprise that in these cases the operations have been judged to be failures.

The major attempt to date to develop an international policy framework for such interventions was the position paper, *An Agenda for Peace*, prepared for the Security Council by the former UN Secretary-General, Boutros Boutros-Ghali (1992). The paper identified four measures the UN might take in response to actual or emerging conflicts:

- *Preventive diplomacy* — This involves diplomatic action, generally taken at the earliest possible opportunity and aimed at preventing disputes from arising between parties and at containing or resolving disputes before they reach the conflict stage. Article 33 of the UN Charter describes a number of available instruments, including negotiation, enquiry, mediation, conciliation, arbitration, judicial settlement, and resort to regional agencies or agreements or other peaceful means.

- *Peacemaking* — This was defined (Boutros-Ghali 1992, p. 11) as "action to bring hostile parties to agreement, essentially through peaceful means foreseen in Chapter VI of the Charter of the UN." Boutros-Ghali's recommendations focused on mediation and negotiation, greater use of the World Court, and the amelioration of situations of potential conflict through international assistance in, for example, the resettlement of displaced persons. These constitute the same methods as described above in article 33 of the UN Charter for preventive diplomacy, but they are applied after a dispute has crossed the threshold into armed conflict. It is also common (Evans 1993) to differentiate between stage-I peacemaking efforts, which aim directly at the cessation of hostilities and stabilization of the situation on the ground, and stage-II efforts, which aim at securing a durable political settlement and may be undertaken in parallel with peacekeeping efforts.

- *Peacekeeping*—This was described (Boutros-Ghali 1992, p. 11) as "the deployment of a UN presence in the field, hitherto with the consent of all the parties concerned, normally involving UN military and/or police personnel and, frequently, civilians as well." This passage alludes to the recent expansion of peacekeeping activities to include nonmilitary activities. In *Supplement to An Agenda for Peace*, Boutros-Ghali (1995) described recent mandates that led peacekeeping operations to forfeit three "particularly important principles," namely, consent of the parties, impartiality, and the nonuse of force except in self-defence: "these have been the tasks of protecting humanitarian operations during continuing warfare, protecting civilian populations in designated safe areas, and pressing the parties to achieve national reconciliation at a pace faster than they were ready to accept" (Boutros-Ghali 1995, para. 34).

  In the same document, Boutros-Ghali (1995, para. 36) argued for a clear distinction between peacekeeping and enforcement action: "peacekeeping and the use of force (other than in self-defense) should be seen as alternative techniques and not as adjacent points on a continuum, permitting easy transition from one to another."

- *Peacebuilding*—This was an important addition made by the Secretary-General to the sequence of conflict-controlling mechanisms at the disposal of the UN. The term refers to strategies aimed at ensuring that disputes and armed conflicts do not arise in the first place or, if do they arise, that they do not recur (Evans 1993). The idea is to prevent the recurrence of violence by moving beyond remedial measures and venturing into the broad area linking conflict with economic and social development. *Peacebuilding* refers to national and international efforts to foster economic development, institution-building, and civil society, in other words, the creation of stable and sustainable states. Preconflict peacebuilding concerns long-term social, economic, and political strategies to help states deal with emerging threats and disputes. By contrast, postconflict peacebuilding involves rehabilitation and reconstruction, institution-building, and specific programs for such purposes as de-mining.

Each of the four measures addresses a particular stage in a conflict's developmental cycle: preventive diplomacy is undertaken during the build-up to conflict but before armed conflict erupts; peacemaking and peacekeeping are undertaken after a conflict has crossed the threshold of armed hostilities; and peacebuilding may be undertaken in the preconflict stage or, as emphasized in *An Agenda for Peace* (Boutros-Ghali 1992), after a conflict or crisis, to help ensure there is no recurrence. Collectively, the four measures are intended to be a more or less comprehensive system for conflict resolution and prevention, and it is this full range of interventions that is meant to be covered by the term *missions for peace*.

An Agenda for Peace advanced a broad approach to security, emphasizing that conflict is often the consequence of human underdevelopment: social injustice, political oppression, poverty, and economic despair (Boutros-Ghali 1992, p. 2):

> *The sources of conflict and war are pervasive and deep. To reach them will require our utmost effort to enhance respect for human rights and fundamental freedoms, to promote sustainable economic and social development for wider prosperity, to alleviate distress and to curtail the existence and use of massively destructive weapons.*

Useful as it is, Boutros-Ghali's position paper contains a number of conceptual ambiguities and contradictions. One is the Secretary-General's adherence to the concept of state sovereignty, despite an acknowledgment of the erosion of sovereignty in the post-Cold War era. One critic pointed out that the paper neglects to mention those cases in which sovereignty is "superseded by new international forms of behaviour just as it is in global environmental politics or finance" (Weiss 1993, p. 8). The actions in Bosnia and Somalia certainly departed from traditional practice: "in neither case was international intervention grounded on self-defense or consent; in both cases the grounds were largely, if not entirely, humanitarian" (Jackson 1993, p. 604).

Jackson (1993, p. 583) outlined three justifications for overriding the principle of nonintervention:

> *(1) self-defence: the intervention is taken for valid reasons of national security or intervention is taken for valid reasons of national security or international peace and security; (2) consent: the intervention is at the request of the government of the target state — perhaps to assist that government to counter a prior intervention or to defend itself against an armed rebellion; (3) humanitarianism: the intervention is to protect the civilian population of the target state (or segments of it) from grave abuses at the hands of its own government or anti-government guerrillas or as a result of domestic anarchy.*

In Bosnia and Somalia, the concept of state sovereignty was inapplicable. Nevertheless, there appeared to be a demand for international organizations to impinge on what, until that time, had been regarded as the sovereign rights of governments. In short, the general good (international peace and security) requires some curtailment of national sovereignty.

Another limitation of Boutros-Ghali's (1992) *An Agenda for Peace* is that the primary focus in securing peace is on the state. The rather perfunctory treatment of the role of NGOs, for example, reflects the tension that persists between the UN and the NGO community. Yet, the involvement of NGOs is essential to mounting successful missions for peace; "conflict management must be conceived broadly enough to include a host of such non-governmental actors as clans and the International Committee of the Red Cross" (Weiss 1993, p. 8). The challenge of the new era is to sort out the roles of different actors in light of their respective interests and capabilities. Boutros-Ghali paid little attention to the interrelationship of the various components of the peace process or to the optimum division of labour. The peacebuilding process seems particularly well suited to NGOs; peacemaking seems essentially a diplomatic–political activity; and peacekeeping, in its traditional sense, is chiefly a military activity.

The multiplicity of mission objectives poses a still more difficult issue. By their very nature, conflict situations send urgent but often contradictory messages, to which is added a cacophony of external voices and interests. In Rwanda, for example, the priorities were to feed needy people, stop the killing, deny legitimacy and impunity to the mass killers, prevent flows of refugees, obtain a cease-fire, and obtain a political settlement. As the case studies in this book make clear, failure to define objectives has been one of the greatest weaknesses of missions for peace.

Defining missions for peace

Missions for peace is not a recognized term in the lexicon of international relations. The generic term the UN uses to encompass its expanded range of interventions is *peace operations.* However, these UN operations always involve the military, which gives short shrift to peace-building, as well as to other activities that do not necessarily involve the military at all. Accordingly, we coined the term *missions for peace* to describe a wide spectrum of multilateral and multidimensional engagements, involving both civil and military elements, that have been developed in an effort to prevent, contain, or resolve conflict. Missions for peace are especially, but not necessarily, associated with the UN, the world's principal multilateral instrument for the maintenance of international peace and security. They are also almost invariably led by countries of the developed or industrialized world, so they tend to reflect the values of Western or liberal-democratic societies.

Such missions are often regarded as an outgrowth of the Cold War innovation of peacekeeping, and peacekeeping is certainly a component. But in many respects, this is an unhelpful connection that has been made simply because peacekeeping has been the chief form of UN intervention and one in which Canada has developed a substantial expertise and reputation. Classical peacekeeping conformed to rather rigid rules: consent of the parties involved in the conflict; use of lightly armed infantry units and limited logistical support; use of weapons only for self-defence; and highly restrictive rules of engagement, the guidelines for soldiers' use of force.

By contrast, missions for peace cover a range of interventions apart from traditional peacekeeping. Their objectives are multiple and, therefore, often ambitious and complex; the interval of intervention is potentially longer; and they are multidimensional, sometimes involving the military but also calling on a variety of civilian skills and expertise. Such missions may now include monitoring of elections, training of civilian police forces, maintenance of law and order, protection of human rights, provision of safe conduct for refugees, development efforts, restoration of infrastructure, de-mining, and humanitarian activities. They are nothing if not ambitious, and the international community is just beginning to learn what makes certain interventions work and what makes others problematic to the point of failure. The issue of objectives has already been mentioned: these multilateral responses attempt to address the underlying causes of conflict, in the hope that a firmer foundation will be laid for durable peace. This is a bold ambition and the subject of considerable controversy.

Traces of an earlier way of thinking about international relations can be found in the concept of missions for peace. Their appeal to Canada arises still from the opportunity they afford to project Canadian values abroad. They build on two Canadian foreign-policy vocations, at least as they evolved during the Cold War: peacekeeping and development assistance. They reflect the now general acceptance of the interrelatedness of the various components of the peace process, both at the conceptual level and at the practical level. In policy terms, this should translate into greater congruence between formerly discrete elements in Canadian foreign policy, specifically peacekeeping and development assistance. In operational terms, missions for peace represent a hybrid of diplomatic and military conflict-resolution techniques, on the one hand, and international-development concerns applied to situations of conflict, on the other.

THE CHANGING INTERNATIONAL CLIMATE

Conceptually appealing as missions for peace may be, there is at present no policy or strategy for where or when they should take place. UN peace operations have been largely reactive, responding only after international media and public opinion have generated strong pressure. A more rational and comprehensive system of engagement remains at best a gleam in the eye of a few middle powers like Canada. To be sure, *An Agenda for Peace* (Boutros-Ghali 1992) generated a fair bit of interest and remains a key document in multilateral maintenance of international peace and security. Boutros-Ghali (1995, para. 44) even mused about the possibility of a rapid-reaction force for the UN:

> *Such a force would be the Security Council's strategic reserve for deployment when there was an emergency need for peace-keeping troops. It might comprise battalion-sized units from a number of countries. These units would be trained to the same standards, use the same operating procedures, be equipped with integrated communications equipment, and take part in joint exercises at regular intervals. They would be stationed in their home countries but maintained at a high state of readiness.*

Three member states — Canada, Denmark, and the Netherlands — all prepared studies on various aspects of the concept of rapid reaction. Canada's study was the most comprehensive; it shrewdly contained a number of relatively modest and practical suggestions for improving UN operations, and so it has elicited considerable interest and some action. Yet, the central idea appears for now to be a nonstarter, not unlike Security Council reform: a laudable notion but unattainable in the current climate.

At the UN the climate has changed from the brief euphoria of the early 1990s to an atmosphere of caution and diminished expectations. This reflects contemporary realities, in which the major powers appear to be retrenching in various areas of the world. They are no longer willing or able "to intervene unilaterally with arms or military forces in proxy wars or conflicts far from home" (Diehl 1993, p. 1). Nor are the major powers eager to consider bold new multilateral initiatives, as they are fatigued and rather sceptical from operations already undertaken, and the Cold War no longer provides the glue or the framework that justifies a common and concerted approach to international problems. The notion of a public good has come under sustained assault in Western societies in recent years, and this trend is paralleled on the international scene by increased doubt and scepticism about investments in common interests such as development assistance. There is far less conviction today that national self-interest requires investment in international or multilateral causes. Other factors, such as financial constraints and increasing social problems within donor countries, have further weakened the attention given to problems abroad.

Virtually all donor countries are reducing their levels of official development assistance (ODA), creating a serious development-aid crisis. Many developing countries no longer have the geopolitical significance they enjoyed during the era of bipolar competition, when states were propped up by the superpowers. Developing countries now compete with eastern European states for economic aid, with the latter tending to have stronger political constituencies in donor countries. At the same time, aid is increasingly seen as a question of emergency and humanitarian assistance. Mark Duffield (cited in Pallister 1994, p. 7), senior lecturer in the School of Public Policy at Birmingham University and consultant to the United Nations Children's Fund, made the following comment:

> *What we are seeing is something unique in the history of warfare — the integration of humanitarian aid into the dynamics of conflict. … Conventional wisdom is how and when to intervene. But my view is that relief systems are a symptom of disengagement with the South. Overseas development assistance is either stagnant or declining while humanitarian aid is rising.*

A new political framework for international cooperation is needed. The aid community acknowledges that, given the new international political conditions, a basic restructuring of ODA is necessary. New thinking and strategies in development assistance have emerged around the notion of sustainable human development. It may be that the best that can be hoped for in the medium term is the selective use of multilateral instruments, along with such mechanisms as can be devised to help the international community choose its interventions well. This is what an editor of *Foreign Policy* called "opportunistic idealism," a pragmatic response to the conundrum of UN overstretch (Maynes 1993, p. 20).

The Canadian response

In Canada, the climate of opinion has also changed. The Canadian government is obliged to deal with a much more sceptical public than in the past. Neither peacekeeping nor development assistance is any longer regarded as a panacea, or even as particularly successful. The peace operations in Rwanda, Somalia, and the former Yugoslavia are regarded as extremely flawed at best, and this has done nothing to burnish the image of UN peacekeeping. As for ODA, Canada like other donor countries is suffering from aid fatigue. Canadians feel less certainty than ever about the effectiveness of aid delivery and far more cynicism about the dependency of the beneficiaries, which the upsurge in humanitarian emergencies has only underscored.

Many Canadians are not convinced that we can or should attempt to cure the world's ills. Canada's resources are now stretched to the limit, they claim, and the country should not be in the business of "pouring money down sinkholes." A kinder, gentler way of framing the argument might be to insist that the cutbacks instituted by the government are necessary under the circumstances and that no new expenditures should be contemplated until fiscal order is restored to Canada's own house. The question for those who value Canada's international involvement is whether voices such as these represent the silent majority or merely a disaffected minority.

Canadians also have less assurance today that our troops are ideally suited to the new generation of peacekeeping, as the grinding controversy over the Somalia affair and inquiry demonstrate. It is doubtful that Canadians are entirely comfortable with the expanding scope and changing nature of missions for peace. The fact that times have changed and that a different sort of force may be called for is bound to raise concerns.

These developments are provoking some rethinking of Canada's international involvements and the way these are organized within the federal bureaucracy. During the Cold War, elements of Canada's external relations were distinct, particularly development assistance and peacekeeping. Development assistance has been channeled through the Canadian International Development Agency, whereas peacekeeping activities have been the domain of the Department of Foreign Affairs (policy) and the Department of National Defence (operations). Since the Cold War there has been greater recognition of the interdependence of security and development concerns, and the international political climate has been favourable toward a more integrated approach to conflict situations. Continuing obstacles to cooperation take the form of differing corporate cultures, institutional rivalry, and budgetary battles over a shrinking resource pie (with both defence and aid budgets under the knife).

Nevertheless, the pressures on Canada to rethink its approach to international peace and security and to rationalize its overseas commitments may yet encourage a cooperative approach. This was the approach suggested by the Special Parliamentary Joint Committee Reviewing Canada's Foreign Policy in 1994 (SJCRCFP 1994, p. 19):

> *What Canada can do is to choose when possible those operations which make best use of the things Canadians do best (e.g. highly professional military skills, air transport and traffic control, logistics, engineering and communications, medical teams, policing and civilian mediation). It may be possible, for example, to combine elements of the "vanguard" concept with elements of an enhanced civilian–military approach, so that Canada could help the UN to intervene swiftly, but could then contribute a smaller force to interface with civilian actors for the longer haul. Such an approach would probably mean limiting Canadian involvement to fewer missions but with more significant participation in each.*

To improve cooperation and coordination among the international, national, government, and nongovernment actors, the committee (SJCRCFP 1994, p. 19) cited suggestions made by a witness for "a program of personnel secondments, a systematic exchange of information, and the establishment of an ongoing tripartite liaison body or roundtable to follow Canada's participation in recent humanitarian operations." A brief prepared by CARE Canada (Cooperative for American Relief Everywhere) urged a rational division of labour among people with the skills and specialities and the organizations currently participating in such missions (CARE Canada 1994; see also Schmite 1995). Thus far, none of these suggestions have been taken up.

For the Chrétien government, cutting the deficit has taken precedence over other considerations. Net ODA decreased from $2.5 billion in the 1993/94 fiscal year to $2.1 billion in the 1996/97 fiscal year, and the government also pared the National Defence budget. At the same time, the government has been actively engaged in thinking about the new generation of peace operations and in participating in several of them. The harrowing experience of Rwanda seared the consciences of a number of highly placed officials. Also, in the government statement on foreign policy, which was tabled in the House of Commons in February 1995, the following reference was made (GOC 1995a, p. 27):

> *Serious shortcomings in UN capabilities ... have been highlighted by slow and hesitant decision-making in the UN that delayed deployment of personnel at the outset of UN involvement in Somalia in 1992, and again in Rwanda in the spring of 1994, when urgent reinforcement of the UN's presence on the ground could not be achieved in time to forestall massive loss of life.*

Out of this experience came the government's decision to undertake a study of a UN rapid-reaction capability. Foreign Minister André Ouellet (1994) told the UN General Assembly that "recent peacekeeping missions have shown that the traditional approach no longer applies." The study, presented to the UN in September 1994, recommended closer civil–military cooperation in pursuit of common goals in future missions (GOC 1995b, p. 66):

> *The more complex missions of the 1990s have already demonstrated the importance of a comprehensive approach to peacekeeping, in which military and civilian staffs, drawn from a number of organizations and agencies, some governmental, some inter-governmental, some non-governmental, work to common objectives. Peacekeeping is no longer a purely military vocation, and humanitarian assistance, legal affairs, human rights, electoral assistance, and other elements have become integral parts of the peacekeeping equation.*

In addition, Canada has been actively engaged in a variety of operations to restore democracy and to assist in institution-building. In Haiti, Canada initially participated in an international maritime embargo to ensure that cargo bound for the country did not violate UN sanctions. Since then Canadian troops, police, and civilians have been involved in leadership roles in efforts to assist the Haitian government in the professionalization of its police, maintenance of a secure environment, national reconciliation, and economic rehabilitation.

These efforts have been clear instances of the government's and particularly Foreign Minister Lloyd Axworthy's keen interest in peacebuilding.

The Canadian government also contributed significantly to the UN multinational force organized in late November and early December 1996 in a desperate effort to avert a major human tragedy in Zaire. This mission was intended to facilitate the delivery of humanitarian aid by relief organizations, as well as to facilitate the voluntary repatriation of refugees and the return of displaced persons by the UN High Commissioner for Refugees. With the massive voluntary flow of refugees from Zaire back to Rwanda, however, the mission's mandate was undermined, and the force was disbanded. According to *The New York Times* (DePalma 1997, p. 16), "there were clear signs that troops were not properly trained or equipped for the task, and officials breathed a sigh of relief when the mission was called off."

Foreign Minister Axworthy, in a speech at York University on 30 October 1996, provided some insights into his approach to the new concept of peacebuilding. The Minister observed that the international community had begun to reconsider the whole concept of security and that out of this two key concepts had emerged: human security and peacebuilding. The former embraces "fundamental freedoms, rule of law, good governance, sustainable development and social equity" (Axworthy 1996). He made the point that if peace is to be restored and sustained, human security must be guaranteed every bit as much as military security is. Peacebuilding enters the picture at this point, described as a "package of measures" to strengthen and solidify peace by "building a sustainable infrastructure of human security" (Axworthy 1996). It aims to put in place the minimal conditions under which a country can take charge of its own destiny and under which social, political, and economic development becomes a possibility (Axworthy 1996):

> *I see peacebuilding as casting a lifeline to foundering societies struggling to end the cycle of violence, restore civility and get back on their feet. After the fighting has stopped and the immediate humanitarian needs have been addressed, there exists a brief critical period when a country sits balanced on a fulcrum. Tilted the wrong way, it retreats into conflict. But with the right help, delivered during that brief, critical window of opportunity, it will move towards peace and stability.*

Axworthy's speech left hanging a fundamental question: Is peacebuilding simply development cooperation under the extreme circumstances of war or is it a new form of emergency assistance that specializes in rebuilding social and political infrastructure? In his speech, the Minister leaned toward the latter view. This would seem to be confirmed by discussions he conducted with the Japanese in April 1997 about the possibility of civilian rapid-response teams as a counterpart to a UN military rapid-reaction capability (McKenna 1997). Such an undertaking could include collaboration on joint training of local police, judges, and human-rights monitors or administrators. Axworthy was quoted (McKenna 1997) as saying that "unless there is the capacity to quickly get engaged after a cease-fire, you then lose whatever momentum there is and a lot of the problems reemerge."

Nevertheless, experience teaches us to be very modest in our expectations of how much difference peacebuilding will make to countries in conflict. In the main, peacebuilding should be seen as the continuation of development assistance in circumstances of deadly conflict. Seen in this light, it is not something new or original: it finds its roots in the period of reconstruction and development after World War II, the most successful experiment in peacebuilding, bar none. The lessons from that period serve as a sobering reminder of what we can expect from contemporary peacebuilding activities. Political will and policy coherence are essential. Moreover, peacebuilding works best when married to economic recovery and large, sustained infusions of outside assistance. The fact that these conditions do not normally obtain in contemporary peacebuilding reminds us that the modesty of our expectations is unavoidable.

The case studies

The case studies that follow were conducted in the context of the changing international climate to which we referred earlier, namely, a more sober, morning-after appreciation of the constraints on missions for peace. The idealism that was embodied in these international interventions has now met repeated, harsh tests of reality arising from, among other things, obdurate forces of history, shifting and contradictory foreign-policy objectives, and organizational roadblocks and potholes. The earlier hope that the international community could put together a conflict-resolution toolbox now seems rather naive.

The purpose of the case studies was to explore the lessons that may be learned from three of the missions for peace that engaged the international community in the past 10 years, namely, Nicaragua, Cambodia, and Somalia. All three missions contributed to the development of a more sober assessment of the prospects for international interventions to end conflict and make peace. We asked each of the authors to provide a general review of the missions for peace while focusing their attention on what they regard as a critical determining factor in shaping such missions.

In the first of the case studies, Andrés Pérez argues that the historical roots of conflict — and the historical constraints on peace — must be understood if the international community is to have any chance to meaningfully contribute to the resolution of conflict. In the case of Nicaragua, the long history of outside intervention in the internal politics of the country has meant that a genuine national politics of negotiation and accommodation was never able to develop. Professor Pérez dwells on this point because, as he argues, missions for peace tend to rest on a naive faith in techniques such as peacekeeping and development assistance as instruments for overcoming history. In place of this historical conceit, he offers this more modest hope (Pérez, this volume, p. 23):

> *A mission for peace should not be conceived of as a form of intervention designed to solve the social, political, and economic problems of a polarized society. The most that missions for peace can hope to achieve is the deactivation of destructive historical forces and their temporary reorientation to more manageable levels. By doing this, missions for peace create new historical opportunities that the elites of politically polarized and socially divided societies can use to begin to construct a minimum social consensus as the foundation of a durable peace.*

In the second of our case studies, Gérard Hervouët explores the connections between Canada's active but modest participation in the UN operation in Cambodia and its wider foreign-policy ambitions. He writes (Hervouët, this volume, p. 58) that

> *as the 1980s drew to a close, it was becoming evident that Canadian interest in a peaceful solution in Cambodia went beyond Khmer borders. Canada's goals were twofold: to increase its participation in ASEAN [Association of Southeast Asian Nations] economic prosperity and simultaneously to position itself in the face of the possible reintegration of Viet Nam into the Southeast Asian economic-expansion zone.*

In documenting Canada's determination to do well while doing good, Professor Hervouët is drawing our attention to the fact that national foreign policies supply much of the motive power behind missions for peace. This elementary point bears repeating because the notion has taken hold in some quarters that missions for peace, particularly UN missions, are powered from some global command post that will soon be running the world.

A mission for peace might be defined as a situation in which the irresistible forces of international politics meet the immovable objects of local history, a point captured perfectly in the title of the third of our case studies "Somalia: When Two Anarchies Meet." The author, Kenneth D. Bush, writes (this volume, p. 93) that "the dynamics of conflict among clans and subclans in Somalia was mirrored in less violent ways in the relations between the international actors involved in relief operations, especially those under the auspices of the UN." His case study documents abundantly that missions for peace are themselves rich sources of conflict as local and international actors compete for resources and power.

In exploring the underlying factors shaping missions for peace, all three of the case studies refer in varying degrees to the Canadian experience. This is not because Canada was the dominant player in any of the missions. Far from it. Partly it is because we are Canadians and naturally draw on the experience of our own country, but there is more to it than that. Few countries in the world have invested more hope than Canada in the promise of missions for peace. These complex undertakings have been seen by some Canadians as a new foreign-policy vocation combining and perhaps superseding the two main foreign-policy vocations of the past 40 years, namely, peacekeeping and development assistance. The tough lessons of the past 10 years have diminished, if not extinguished, those hopes.

We fear Canadians are in danger of learning the lessons too well and concluding that their country's foreign policy should be far more self-interested than it already is. It is true that the record of missions for peace is a cautionary tale for enthusiastic, or at least naive, internationalism. It is equally true, however, that the lessons point to the continuing need for effective internationalism. Each of our case studies begins with a situation of persistent conflict generating enormous human suffering for the people of a country and instability for the international community. In all of these cases, the level of conflict and suffering was much diminished after international intervention, although, as recent events in Cambodia reveal, the situation on the ground is still well short of paradise. We argue that the lesson of these cases studies is that we can and should learn to conduct missions for peace more effectively, not that we should abandon the effort.

Chapter 2

Nicaragua

History, social conflict, and missions for peace

Andrés Pérez

A mission for peace is an initiative "launched during a violent conflict which seeks to foster and support sustainable structures and processes which strengthen the prospects for peaceful coexistence and decrease the likelihood of the outbreak (or reoccurrence) of violent conflict" (Bush 1994, p. 1). The conflicts that missions for peace try to resolve are usually caused by institutionalized social tensions and contradictions. The processes whereby these tensions and contradictions generate violent conflict remain controversial and complex subjects of inquiry. Equally complex is the phenomenon of the rearticulation of peace and its subsequent maintenance. This complexity is not well understood in current discussions of missions for peace, which tend to provide mainly ahistorical and voluntaristic analyses of social phenomena. These analyses emphasize political will, political motivation, and political decisions as the main factors determining the impact of these missions. These analyses fail to grasp the complex relationship between political agency and the structural and historical limitations affecting the impact of missions for peace.

The ahistorical and voluntaristic approach, characteristic of conventional interpretations of missions for peace, has resulted in a distorted view of their potential and actual contributions to world peace. This distortion is reflected in the inflation of the concept of missions for peace, which demonstrates impatience with historical complexity and a desire to apply holistic solutions to the problems of politically polarized and socially divided societies.

Previously, politicians and analysts spoke of "peacekeeping," "peaceobserving," and "peacemaking." Increasingly, missions for peace hope to offer all these, plus "peacebuilding," which is a central element of *An Agenda for Peace* (Boutros-Ghali 1992). Peacebuilding has been defined as "the development effort that attempts to reduce conflict by improving social and economic conditions and meeting fundamental human needs" (Child 1992, p. 3). The central assumption behind this idea is that "economic and social injustices must be addressed in order to provide the basis for a permanent solution to conflict" (Child 1992, p. 3). To assume that missions for peace should include provisions to resolve institutionalized social tensions and contradictions in war-torn societies is unrealistic. This is especially true today, when the demand for peace intervention seems to be exceeding the financial capabilities of the leading peacekeeping countries (Gizewski and Pearson 1993).

The inflation of the concept of missions for peace has resulted in the amalgamation of social variables and institutional mandates under the truism that everything is interrelated. The idea and practice of development, for example, have been transformed into a "phase" of the peace process (Cox 1993, p. 8). Never mind if this is the final phase, the longest phase, or the phase that nobody knows how to deal with. This mixing up of variables and institutional mandates has its dangers. The increasingly unrealistic expectations that social scientists, politicians, social activists, and the public have of missions for peace may lead to the failure (perceived or real) of these initiatives. The result of this failure could be the invalidation of the important functions of peacekeeping, peaceobserving, and peacemaking. Another possible danger is the illusion of order and accomplishment that an all-inclusive concept of missions for peace can create among government and international organizations. Often, these organizations assume that they shift and rearrange reality by shifting and rearranging concepts and that a more inclusive concept of missions for peace represents a better understanding of the world.

One can speculate that the tendency to inflate the concept of missions for peace has more to do with the organizational needs of the institutions involved in these missions than with the need to understand the nature of social conflict in war-torn societies. These institutions need to demonstrate that they are capable of coordinating their role and their functions to match the complexity of the processes in which they operate. They need to demonstrate that they know what they are doing. All this is perfectly understandable. What is not understandable or acceptable is to forget that the resolution of institutional problems is very different from the resolution of the conundrum of history and development in war-torn societies.

The main argument of this chapter is that a mission for peace should not be conceived of as a form of intervention designed to solve the social, political, and economic problems of a polarized society. The most that missions for peace can hope to achieve is the deactivation of destructive historical forces and their temporary reorientation to more manageable levels. By doing this, missions for peace create new historical opportunities that the elites of politically polarized and socially divided societies can use to begin to construct a minimum social consensus as the foundation of a durable peace.

In this chapter, a case study of the Nicaraguan peace process is used as the basis for an analysis of the role of missions for peace in the reconstruction of social processes. The first section reviews the institutionalization of the social tensions and contradictions that formed the background to the Contra War. The second section reviews the Central American peace process as it applied to Nicaragua; the purpose of this section is to show the interplay of political agency, domestic historical forces, and external conditions that resulted in the signing and implementation of the peace accords. The third section analyzes the nature of the peace achieved in Nicaragua. This analysis forms the foundation for the fourth section, which evaluates the Central American peace process and the mission for peace in Nicaragua and presents some lessons for Canada.

Agency and structure in the history of political conflict and political change in Nicaragua

Social peace depends to a large extent on a minimal social consensus on the organization of political conflict (see Sartori 1987). The institutionalization of consensus, which in liberal-democratic countries is an expression of the correlation of forces among domestic power contenders, has never had a chance in Nicaragua. Throughout this century, US governments have, by their "acts of commission and omission" (Whitehead 1986, p. 230), formed artificial domestic alliances, switched the correlation of power within the country, supported dictatorial and illegitimate governments, eliminated political forces, and created new ones to force Nicaragua's political evolution to conform to American political objectives, policies, and strategies for the region.

Determining the political development of Nicaragua has been a perpetual dilemma for US governments. American democratic traditions and institutions required that interventions in Nicaragua be justified by the same principles that rationalize political life in the United States. Thus, the principles of democracy had to be used to legitimize US interventions in Nicaragua. However, democracy creates uncertainty (Przeworski 1986), and this does not sit well with the overwhelming desire for certainty that the United States has traditionally shown in its relations with Nicaragua. US governments, therefore, have conveniently interpreted and manipulated the meaning and practice of democracy, particularly the meaning and practice of elections, to overcome this dilemma. In so doing, they have severely impeded Nicaragua's ability to create a social consensus with regard to the rules that govern political life and political competition.

One of the legacies of US interventionism in Nicaragua is the development and institutionalization of a political culture in which alliances between national groups and foreign interventionist powers have displaced internal discussion and compromise as mechanisms for conflict resolution. For this reason, the independent exploration of political options has not found fertile soil in this country — political decisions have largely been made at foreign embassies and at foreign capital cities.

The mission for peace in Nicaragua was hampered not only by Washington's historical perception of Nicaragua as part of its backyard and by the virulent anti-Americanism of the Sandinistas but also by a political culture in which domestic politics was perceived as a by-product of alliances between national power contenders and their external supporters. The following is a review of the political history of Nicaragua that explains the complexity of this culture and the nature of the historical forces that conditioned the work of the mission for peace in this country. This review is necessary because it helps to transcend the ahistorical and voluntaristic interpretations of social conflict and social order in conventional analyses of missions for peace. It is offered as a reminder that "what is past is prologue" (*The Tempest*, Act II, Scene 1 [William Shakespeare]) and that missions for peace have limited capacities to transform the historical and structural conditions in which social disorder and violent conflicts take place.

The United Kingdom was the most influential external power in the political development of Central America during the first three decades of its independent life, particularly during the federalist experiment. In Nicaragua, this began to change with the expansionist policies of the James Knox Polk Administration (1845–49), the discovery of gold in California in 1848, and the emerging need for cross-continental transportation routes (Karnes 1961). The gold mines in California made the Rio San Juan interoceanic route in Nicaragua a valuable asset, and consequently it became a source of tension between the United Kingdom and the United States. In 1850, they signed the Clayton–Bulwer Treaty, which guaranteed cooperation between the two countries and established that neither would have exclusive control of the Nicaraguan interoceanic route. Nevertheless, the United Kingdom maintained control of large areas of Nicaragua's Atlantic coast.

The Clayton–Bulwer Treaty marked the beginning of the decline of the United Kingdom's influence in Nicaragua and the rise of the United States as the most important external force shaping the political evolution of this Central American country (LaFeber 1984). Henceforth, Nicaraguan domestic politics would be shaped by US pressure to accommodate US interests, and Nicaraguan politicians would be unable and often unwilling to resolve their differences within the legal and political boundaries of Nicaragua as a sovereign state. This became painfully evident during the civil war of 1854, fought between the Liberals and the Conservatives for control of the state and, more specifically, for control of the transisthmian route developed and exploited by the US transportation magnate, Cornelius Vanderbilt (Vazquez 1983; Slotkin 1985).

The Liberals hired William Walker, a "filibuster" from Nashville, Tennessee, and 55 mercenaries to fight the Conservatives. Filibusters, as Slotkin (1985, p. 243) explained, "were private military expeditions, usually invited and organized by Latin American patriots-in-exile or embattled in-country partisans, whose aim was to use American manpower and firepower to achieve victory." Earlier, Walker had led a failed expedition with the objective of creating a slave state out of Lower California and Sonora (Morison et al. 1980). In Nicaragua, however, he proved that he had what Slotkin (1985, p. 244) described as a filibuster's most important qualification: "the ability to act swiftly and decisively, making the maximum use of temporary military advantage to create a political *fait accompli*."

Walker's forces defeated the Conservative army and, with the collaboration of members of the Nicaraguan elite, gained control of the country. He changed the Nicaraguan electoral system — which since independence had restricted political competition and political participation to a small segment of society — and allowed mass participation. (For a description of electoral procedures and regulations in Nicaragua before the 1856 elections, see Alvarez Lejarza [1958].) In 1856, Walker stood for office, manipulated the electoral process, and became the head of government. (For analyses of the illegitimate and fraudulent nature of this election, see Scrooggs [1969]; Bermann [1986]; Torres Rivas [1987].) As President, Walker made English an official language, promulgated laws to establish peonage and slavery in the country, and encouraged immigration from Europe and the United States.

Apart from Walker's popularity in the United States and the strong support he received from some US organizations, the questions most relevant to understanding Nicaragua's political development in the mid-19th century are the following: How did Walker manage to radically alter the rules of political competition in Nicaragua? How could he have gained collaboration from important sectors of the country's elite? Bermann (1986, p. 58) asked this question and provided an answer to it:

> *How could a small handful of North American adventurers, virtually overnight, take control of an independent nation? Luck, superior armaments, the shortage of professional officers among the native troops — all these played a role, but were not decisive. The most important part of the answer lay in the conditions of Nicaraguan politics.*

Torres Rivas (1987, p. 80) proposed a similar inquiry: "We should inquire into the cultural, political, and economic meaning of the ritual by which authority was transferred from the Nicaraguan provisional President Ferrer to the American filibuster Walker." Answers to these questions are to be found in the weakness of Nicaragua's political formation, that is, in the absence of national values and national institutions and in the "predominance of regional and particular interests over national ones" (Lanuza 1983, p. 100).

Walker's presence in Nicaragua, together with his expansionist ambitions, threatened the Central American oligarchies, who united against the US adventurer and managed to drive him out of Nicaragua in 1857. It is important to note that Walker's defeat was possible only with the assistance of the United Kingdom and Cornelius Vanderbilt. The recourse to foreign assistance — this time to oust Walker — was a clear example both of Central America's weakness and of Nicaragua's frailty as a nation-state (Morison et al. 1980; LaFeber 1984). Walker's defeat marked the beginning of 36 years of oligarchical Conservative rule and relatively stable electoral politics in Nicaragua. The constitution of 1858 reestablished capital and property requirements for participation in competition for public office (Alvarez Lejarza 1958).

At the turn of the century, new tensions developed between the Conservative oligarchy and the Liberal elites as the latter's economic capabilities expanded with Nicaragua's integration into the international coffee market. These tensions created the conditions for the successful Liberal revolution of 1893, led by Jose Santos Zelaya (Wheelock 1980; Vargas 1990). (For a vivid description of the social and political life of Nicaragua during the emergence of the Zelaya government, see Selva [1948].)

Zelaya, who represented the interests of the elites associated with the coffee business, transformed the social and political structure of the country to suit its new economic reality. He developed the basic financial and physical infrastructure necessary to encourage the production, processing, and export of coffee. These changes were accompanied by a radical transformation of the country's legal structure and by the organization of a strong central state apparatus. Social services and a public education system were established, and universal suffrage was introduced (Vargas 1990).

Zelaya was a nationalist dictator, as well as being a social reformer. In 1894, with the support of the United States, he recovered the areas of Nicaragua's Atlantic coast controlled by the United Kingdom and reasserted the territorial integrity of the Nicaraguan state. The United States tolerated Zelaya's nationalism as long as it was directed against the United Kingdom but considered it an intolerable menace when it began to affect US interests in the region (Barahona 1977). It is interesting to note, however, that Selser (1984) cast some doubts on Zelaya's nationalism and anti-imperialism. Cancellation of some concessions to American businesses on the Atlantic coast, the rejection of the financial conditions imposed by US bankers, Zelaya's decision to obtain financial assistance from the Ethelburg Syndicate of England, and more importantly his intention to negotiate the construction of a canal through Nicaragua with Germany and Japan convinced Washington that this Nicaraguan government was a threat to US interests. The US solution was to instigate Zelaya's overthrow by supporting an armed counterreformist Conservative movement, which won power in 1910. Vargas (1989, p. 142) argued that the overthrow of the Zelaya regime "castrated the possibility to consolidate a Nicaraguan nation-state."

The persistence of Liberal nationalist forces in the country and the Conservatives' incapacity to consolidate their power after Zelaya's overthrow prompted the United States to occupy Nicaragua in August 1912. First, US marines forced the Liberal troops in Granada to surrender. Then, on 4 October, they launched a decisive attack against the army, which was commanded by General Benjamin Zeledon and positioned on Coyotepe Hill outside the city of Masaya (Millet 1977). Zeledon refused to surrender and died "in defense of his country, of his army, and of his race" (Wheelock 1980, pp. 110–111). His body was paraded through the streets of Masaya and buried in the town of Catarina.

US-controlled presidential elections were held in 1912, 1916, 1920, 1924, and 1928. (For analyses of these elections, see USDS [1932], Envío [1984], and Vargas [1989].) The Liberals were not allowed to stand for the 1912 and 1916 elections, which ensured victories for Conservative, prointerventionist presidents. The exclusion of Liberals was in accordance with the US State Department's written disapproval of "any revival of Zelayaism" (USDS 1932, p. 21). Washington's decision to exclude the Liberals from political competition was ratified by Nicaragua in Agreement No. 4 of the Dawson pacts, signed on 27 October 1910.

The Liberals were allowed to participate in the 1920 election and, following the 1924 election, were able to join a Government of Reconciliation. This election was held within the framework of a new electoral law approved by the Nicaraguan Congress in 1923 (Greer 1954; Kamman 1968). It is important to point out that by 1920, the Liberal Party had practically abandoned Zelaya's nationalist position (Vargas 1989). In the preceding 10 years, the United States had succeeded in changing the political orientation of the party. This process of political sterilization reached its apex three decades later, when the Somozas took control of the political organization.

In 1925, the Government of Reconciliation was overthrown by the Conservative caudillo Emiliano Chamorro. A civil war in 1926 led to another occupation of Nicaragua by the United States, lasting from 1927 to 1933. The United States never recognized Chamorro as president, and he was forced to resign in favour of another Conservative, Adolfo Diaz. This was the second time Washington had selected Adolfo Diaz to be president of Nicaragua. In 1911, he had assumed the presidency after Juan Jose Estrada was invited to resign by Elliot Northcott, the American representative in Nicaragua. Diaz was an accountant for the La Luz and Los Angeles Mining Co. before he became president in 1911. The owners of this company were legally represented in the United States by Secretary of State Philander C. Knox's law firm (Selser 1981). After Diaz was made president, Washington sent Colonel Henry Stimson, a lawyer and former Secretary of War (1911–13) under William H. Taft, to investigate and, if possible, "to straighten" Nicaragua's problems (Stimson 1927, p. 42). Stimson soon managed to pressure the Liberals and Conservatives into a compromise, which resulted in the Stimson–Moncada Pact, better known as the Tipitapa Pact or *Pacto del Espino Negro*. The Conservatives drafted the terms of the pact, and Stimson conveyed the terms to the Liberals. These terms included the following (Stimson 1927):

- Immediate general peace in time for the new crop and delivery of arms simultaneously by both parties to US custody;
- General amnesty, return of exiles, and return of confiscated property;
- Participation of representative Liberals in Diaz's cabinet;
- Organization of a Nicaraguan constabulary on a nonpartisan basis, commanded by US officers;
- Supervision of the election in 1928 and those in succeeding years by Americans, who would have ample police power to make such supervision effective; and
- Temporarily continued presence of a sufficient force of marines to make the foregoing effective.

Jose Maria Moncada, the military commander of the Liberal forces, agreed to these terms of reference, with the exception of the implicit acceptance of the continuation of Adolfo Diaz as President of Nicaragua to the end of his term. Moncada wrote of these negotiations that he had pointed out to Stimson that the US government was making a mistake in allowing the Conservative government of Diaz to continue in power until the 1928 election. According to Moncada (1973, p. 6), Stimson replied, "my government has recognized President Adolfo Diaz and the United States of America does not make mistakes." Augusto Cesar Sandino, who had returned from Mexico in 1926 to join the Liberal forces, refused to accept the pact and went into the Segovia mountains to initiate his heroic anti-interventionist struggle.

The Liberals won the 1928 election. As Vargas (1989) explained, this favoured the United States for at least three reasons: first, a Liberal victory helped neutralize Sandino's cause; second, Moncada's election put the Liberal Party under the control of the United States, which wanted to eliminate the possibility of a nationalist revival within the party; and, third, the election of a Liberal government eliminated the need for the United States to support the unpopular Conservative Party. The Liberals were elected again in 1932. One year later, the US Marines ended their occupation of Nicaragua, thus allowing Sandino to negotiate peace with the government of Juan Bautista Sacasa. Sandino was assassinated in Managua in 1934 during the negotiations.

The regimes of the US-controlled elections of the post-Zelaya era proved to be fragile and artificial solutions to Nicaragua's domestic political problems, as demonstrated by the instability and the high levels of political disorder prevalent in the country after 1910. At least 10 armed rebellions were launched against the Conservative governments between 1913 and 1924 (Wheelock 1980). These governments did not represent the actual balance of power among the different sectors of Nicaraguan society. They were, rather, an expression of the United States' overbearing power, as exercised through Nicaraguan elites, who lacked both the power and the will to lead the economic and political development of their country (Barahona 1977). The United States gained control of Nicaragua's political and economic life through these elites. Furthermore, the Chamorro–Bryan Treaty of 1914 granted the United States perpetual rights to the construction of an interoceanic canal through Nicaragua and a 99-year lease on the Gulf of Fonseca and the Corn Islands.

When the US Marines withdrew from Nicaragua, they left behind the newly created Guardia Nacional (national guard) as Washington's main instrument for maintaining social order. This military organization was placed under the control of the ruthless Anastasio Somoza Garcia, the founder of the Somoza dynasty and the man whom Franklin D. Roosevelt later described as Washington's "son of a bitch"

(Selser 1984, p. 241). Somoza had made a favourable impression on Henry Stimson, who wrote in his diary, "Somoza is a very frank, friendly, likable young Liberal and his attitude impresses me more favourably than almost any other" (Millet 1977, p. 55). In 1936, Stimson's favourite deposed President Sacasa and appointed himself the Liberal Party's official candidate for the election in November of that year. He became the elected president of Nicaragua on 1 January 1937.

Somoza immediately initiated a process of constitutional reform that would allow him to extend his presidential term to 8 years. Master of legal technicalities, he resigned temporarily, appointed himself interim president, organized new elections, then ran for the presidency once again and was elected, through fraud and coercion, with 99% of the vote. (The chronology and data on elections under Somocista rule presented here are mainly based on the excellent account of the Somoza dynasty given by Diederich [1981].)

In the 1947 election, Somoza engineered the victory of his presidential candidate, Leonardo Arguello. Arguello was overthrown by Somoza less than a month after his inauguration. Somoza then installed a new president, deposed him, and finally took direct control of the government himself. The dictator's scandalous political behaviour forced the United States to criticize his electoral abuses. He responded by placing his uncle, Victor Roman Y Reyes, in the presidency. Washington accepted Somoza's concession.

Somoza was elected again in 1951, this time for a period of 6 years, and the constitution was changed before his term was over to allow him to run in the 1957 election. Somoza's presidential career, however, was almost over. On 21 September 1956, the dictator was assassinated by the Nicaraguan poet Rigoberto Lopez Perez. Anastasio Somoza was dead, but the Somoza dynasty was just beginning.

Luis Somoza, Anastasio Somoza's eldest son, was immediately appointed president by the National Congress, with a mandate to finish his father's term. Luis then declared himself the official candidate of the Liberal Party for the 1957 election. He won this election and ruled Nicaragua until 1963. His brother, Anastasio Somoza Jr, was head of the Guardia Nacional. To diffuse domestic and international criticism, the Somozas appointed Rene Schick as the official Liberal candidate for the 1963 election. Schick was elected president; Luis was appointed to the Senate; and Anastasio maintained control of the armed forces.

In March 1966, Anastasio Somoza Jr announced his candidacy for the presidential election of February 1967. He won and was inaugurated for a 4-year term. His brother Luis died of a heart attack in

April of that year. The constitution did not allow Somoza to run for the presidency in the elections of 1972; consequently, he stepped down temporarily while constitutional changes were made to facilitate his reelection later. In the meantime, a Somoza-controlled junta was formed to run the country.

In 1974, Somoza was once again elected president, this time for a 6-year term ending in 1981. Meanwhile, his son, also named Anastasio, was being rushed through the ranks of the national armed forces as part of his preparation for the presidency of Nicaragua. The triumph of the Sandinista Revolution in July 1979 brought a dramatic end to the Somoza dynasty.

The Somozas' power was based on their control of the armed forces, the complicity of the economic elites that benefited from their rule, and above all the political, economic, and military support of successive US governments, which saw the Somozas as protectors of US interests in the region and as bastions against communist penetration in Central America. In this sense, the Somocista regime was the expression of a correlation of domestic political forces determined by the United States. In this externally determined balance of power, elections had no democratic significance, as their results never reflected the actual correlation of political forces in the country. The Somozas manipulated constitutional reforms and the electoral technology of democracy to legalize their illegitimate regime.

The end of Somocista rule and the military victory of the Frente Sandinista de Liberación Nacional (FSLN, Sandinista national liberation front) in 1979 provoked a reaction in Washington similar to that caused by the Zelaya government in 1909. With the socialist Sandinista government, Nicaragua's political future was once again uncertain and once again out of US control. Washington reacted by launching an undeclared war against the Nicaraguan government. An economic embargo was imposed on the small Central American nation, and a series of covert US military operations was carried out in an attempt to overthrow the Sandinista government. Later, a counterrevolutionary army, better known as the Contras, was organized and financed by the United States for the alleged defence of freedom and democracy in Nicaragua.

The Sandinistas' view of the US government was shaped by the historical evolution of relations between Nicaragua and the United States. One of the central principles of the Sandinista revolution was its anti-imperialism. For the Sandinistas, this meant anti-Americanism, as in, for example, the organization's official anthem, which proclaimed the revolutionary obligation "to fight against the Yankee, enemy of humanity."

The Sandinistas organized an election in 1984 in an attempt to undermine Washington's justification of its support of the Contra army. The United States refused to recognize the election because Washington anticipated a Sandinista victory. When the ballots were counted, the Sandinistas had received 66.97% of the vote in an election considered fair and clean by many foreign observers. Washington labeled the election a sham and continued its attacks on the Sandinista government, still hoping that the Contras would make the Sandinistas cry "uncle."

In this context, both regional and extraregional players launched several peace initiatives in Central America. The search for peace in Nicaragua required attempts to negotiate differences between the US and Sandinista governments, as well as negotiating differences between the Sandinistas and their domestic opponents. All this took place in the context both of a history of conflict and aggression between Nicaragua and the United States and of a Nicaraguan political culture unconducive to domestic political negotiations and compromises. This context affected the potential success of any peace initiative and, therefore, had to be taken into consideration by those involved in the peace efforts.

The existence of both institutionalized historical relations between Nicaragua and the United States and a domestic political culture unconducive to peace and social consensus does not mean that the scope of political agency was predetermined by historical forces. Institutionalized social practices should not be seen as placed "beyond the reach of interest and politics" (DiMaggio 1988, p. 11). A depoliticized view of institutionalized patterns of social relations eliminates the possibility of political action in the making of history. Social structures, as Giddens (1984, p. 25) pointed out, "are both medium and outcome of the practices they recursively organize." As outcomes, structures enable and limit political agents; as mediums, they become the vehicle through which societal systems are maintained or changed by such agents (Giddens 1984). This means that "structure *qua structure* does not produce patterns, nor does it actively coordinate and control social systems. All of these activities involve the exercise of agency" (Cohen 1989, p. 199). Agency, then, constitutes the very structures that condition human freedom of action and choice. Therefore, political action can expand the framework of historical limitations and circumstances within which political action takes place. Nevertheless, "to choose a possibility in a given situation is to choose under limits" (Guerreiro Ramos 1981, p. 26). Therefore, "the subject of a choice in a process of change can only be successful if he behaves considering the concrete limitations of his choice" (Guerreiro Ramos 1981, p. 26).

The following section reviews the Central American peace process, especially as it applied in Nicaragua, to highlight the relationship between agency and structure in the search for peace in Central America. Two lessons can be derived from an analysis of this relationship. First, the design and implementation of the Central American peace process required those involved in the mission for peace in Nicaragua to assess both the will of the actors of the region and the way structural conditions — such as the historical relations between Nicaragua and the United States, along with the Nicaraguan political culture — affected the possibilities for peace. Second, an analysis of the relationship between agency and structure in the search for peace in Nicaragua facilitates an understanding of the limited capacity that the mission for peace had to radically transform the structural conditions that generated conflict and war in this country. This understanding is important in view of the tendency of conventional analyses of missions for peace to use ahistorical and voluntaristic interpretations of social phenomena. This chapter has argued that missions for peace should not be conceived of as forms of intervention designed to resolve the social, political, and economic problems of a polarized society. The Nicaraguan case demonstrates that missions for peace should be conceived as forms of interventions designed to create new historical opportunities that the elites of politically polarized and socially divided societies can use to construct a minimum social consensus as a foundation for consolidating order and peace.

The Peace Process

Like Nicaragua, the other Central American countries are plagued by internal social tensions and contradictions and by a history of conflict with the United States. In the 1980s, guerrilla movements in El Salvador and Guatemala, following the example of the Sandinista revolution, were attempting to overthrow the governments of these two countries. Honduras was caught in the middle of the US–Nicaragua conflict, with its territory being used by the Contras as a military base for operations against the Sandinista government. Meanwhile, Costa Rica was under tremendous pressure from Washington to collaborate in the war against the Nicaraguan government; at the same time, Costa Rica was suffering the effects of massive Nicaraguan migration.

Two events marked the opening of this chapter of violence in Central America: the Sandinista victory in July 1979 and the inauguration of Ronald Reagan as President of the United States in January 1980. The Sandinista victory energized popular movements and guerrilla organizations in El Salvador and Guatemala, whereas the advent of the Reagan Administration ideologically, economically, and militarily invigorated the most conservative social sectors of those societies. This dynamic created the conditions for a war that in several instances threatened to engulf the whole region in a spiral of domestic and international confrontation. The first efforts to establish peace in Central America included proposals from Costa Rica, El Salvador, and Honduras in the last months of 1981: Costa Rica's initiative of October 1982; the Plan de Paz proposed by Mexican President José Lopez Portillo in February 1982; and a joint initiative by Mexico and Venezuela, launched in September of the same year (Bernales and Fernandez 1990).

However, a solid, credible, and systematic search for peace in Central America only emerged when the Contadora peace process was initiated by Colombia, Mexico, Panama, and Venezuela on the Panamanian island of Contadora in January 1983. The Contadora process confronted both the political and the military dimensions of the Central American conflict. It included provisions to promote national processes of reconciliation, cease-fires, democratization, free elections, and decrees of amnesty. The Contadora process also proposed that the Central American governments stop assisting irregular forces or insurrectionist movements and using their territories to destabilize other governments in the region and start negotiating on matters of security, verification, control, and limitation of armaments, caring for refugees and displaced persons, and cooperating for peace and development. Finally, the plan established a mechanism for international verification and follow-up of the agreements (Moreno 1994).

From 1984 to 1986, three drafts of this plan were presented to the Central American governments (North 1990). None of these satisfied the demands and expectations of all parties involved because the Contadora process took place at a time when the historical tensions between the United States and Nicaragua were magnified by the Cold War, the fierce anti-Communist position of the Reagan Administration, and the Manichean understanding of international politics espoused by the Sandinistas. In other words, the scope for political compromise and negotiation during this period was severely constrained by the polarization of both domestic political forces in Nicaragua and the relations between the Sandinistas and Washington.

During this process, Nicaragua and the United States each operated under the assumption that it did not have to compromise, as both assumed they would eventually prevail over the other. For example, on 2 December 1985, US Secretary of State George Schultz expressed to the four Contadora ministers that the Sandinista government was a "cancer" that required a "surgical solution" (Sklar 1988, p. 306). Nevertheless, it was necessary for both Nicaragua and the United States to express interest in negotiation, compromise, and peace. Therefore, they agreed on generalities and disagreed on the practical details of peace.

In Nicaragua, the polarization between the Sandinistas and Washington made it impossible to develop a feasible domestic process of political competition in which opposition against the regime was not viewed as collaboration with the United States. Nor was it possible to support the revolution without going along with the fierce anti-American rhetoric of the FSLN. Therefore, to adopt a political position in Nicaragua, one either had to be a collaborator with the United States or had to become anti-American. Furthermore, to be anti-American in Nicaragua meant one was necessarily pro-Soviet, as the logic of "the enemy of my enemy is my friend" was an implicit principle of Sandinismo. Very soon, Nicaraguan domestic politics was subsumed under the logic of the Cold War. Opponents of Sandinismo begged for Washington's support while the leaders of the FSLN negotiated in Moscow to find ways to institutionalize the revolution.

The international and domestic conditions affecting the negotiations and the Contadora process also affected efforts to establish direct negotiation between Nicaragua and the United States. The most significant of these efforts was initiated by Mexico in 1984. This culminated in the Manzanillo talks, which lasted until January 1985, when the United States suspended the bilateral negotiations (Bernales and Fernandez 1990). These direct conversations between Managua and Washington had little chance of success, as the participants still assumed they did not have to compromise on their positions.

At their meeting in June 1986 at Esquipulas, the Central American presidents rejected what would be the last Contadora peace proposal. They condemned the assistance approved by the US Congress to the Contras, declared support for the principles of the Contadora process, and launched a new peace initiative that became known as the Esquipulas process. Launching the Esquipulas process represented the "centroamericanization" of the peace process. This was an important step because it removed nationalist resentments that had been created by the leading roles of extraregional Latin American governments during the Contadora process. More importantly, the centroamericanization of the peace process imposed more direct responsibility for the outcome of the negotiations on the governments of the region. This responsibility required these governments to deal with the tensions that existed between the interests of the United States and those of the people and governments of Central America. These tensions included the increasing fears within the Honduran government and military that the conflict with Nicaragua could result in a war between the two countries; the problem that the continuous military support given by the United States to El Salvadorean armed forces represented for the Honduran military, with El Salvador being viewed by Hondurans as its rival; the concern of the Guatemalan government that the intensification of conflict in the region could exacerbate the domestic problems in that country; and the fear of the Costa Rican government that continuous Nicaraguan immigration and the possible expansion of the war could involve Costa Rica in a regional confrontation. The increasing visibility of these situations helped to develop a degree of political pragmatism among Central American governments that was decisive in the success of the peace process.

The crucial point of departure for the Esquipulas process was the meeting of Central American presidents in Guatemala City, 6–7 August 1987. In essence, Esquipulas was a natural continuation of the principles and objectives of the Contadora peace process, as acknowledged in the preamble to the *Act of Accord* produced at this meeting. Esquipulas proposed the initiation of processes of national reconciliation; amnesty; cessation of hostilities; democratization; free elections; cessation of aid to irregular forces and insurgent movements; nonuse of territory to attack other states; negotiations on security, verification, control, and limitation of weapons; and solutions to the problem of refugees and displaced persons. The implementation of the plan included the establishment of the Comisiones Nacionales de Reconciliación (national reconciliation commissions) in Guatemala, El Salvador, and Nicaragua and the Comisión Internacional de Verificación y Seguimiento (CIVS, International Commission for Verification and Follow-up). The three national reconciliation commissions comprised a representative of the government and an alternate; a representative and an alternate proposed by the Conference of Bishops and chosen by the government from a list of three bishops; a representative and an alternate from opposition political parties; and an eminent citizen and an alternate belonging to neither the government nor the governing party. These commissions were to be responsible for "verifying genuine implementation of the process of national reconciliation and also unrestricted respect for all the civil and political rights of Central American citizens" (Moreno 1994, appendix 5, p. 191). The CIVS comprised the Secretary-General of the United Nations or his representative, the ministers of foreign affairs of Central American countries, and the Contadora group and its support group. The commission was responsible for verifying and monitoring whether the governments were keeping the commitments made in Esquipulas.

Needless to say, the issue of verification was complex and sensitive. The physical conditions for doing the job were extremely difficult. Moreover, the verification of the Esquipulas accord was perceived as a threat by Honduras and the United States, whose anti-Sandinista operations in the region were in direct violation of one of the key clauses of the accord. This clause required the five countries of the region "to prevent the use of their own territory by persons, organizations or groups seeking to destabilize the Governments of Central American countries and to refuse to provide them with or allow them to receive military and logistical support" (Moreno 1994, appendix 5, p. 195).

The first report of the CIVS was presented to the five Central American presidents in January 1988 at San José, Costa Rica. As expected, the report was critical of Honduras and the United States, and it provoked a strong reaction from El Salvador and Honduras, the main US allies in the region. As a result, the work of the commission was suspended, and its members were reduced to the five foreign ministers of Central America (Envío 1989).

The opposition to the verification mechanism of the Esquipulas process highlighted both the superficiality of the peace negotiations and the contradictory positions of the governments. The objective of the verification accord was to change words into deeds, that is, to move from the rhetoric of peace to the actual process of negotiation and compromise that would result in the reduction and possible elimination of conflict. For the United States and its regional allies, the transition from rhetoric to action would be costly, as it would involve the removal of the anti-Sandinista military, their most important negotiating card. For the Sandinistas, on the other hand, verification and the success of the peace process meant at the very least putting an end to their confrontation with the United States and its regional allies. More importantly, it would provide the Sandinistas with an opportunity to control to some extent the domestic crisis in Nicaragua.

In Central America, progress toward compromise and peace required a significant change in the international structures responsible for the polarization of relations between Managua and Washington and of those among Nicaraguan contenders for power. This change came with the rise to power of Mikhail Gorbachev in the Soviet Union. The improvement in relations between the two superpowers initiated by perestroika and glasnost had decisive effects on the Esquipulas peace process. The most dramatic of these were the loss of the Sandinista's symbolic position in the eyes of the US government as regional representatives of the "Evil Empire"; and the reorientation of US foreign-policy priorities away from Central America. At the same time, these events lessened the symbolic and strategic value of the Sandinista government for the Soviet Union. The Soviet Union reduced its political, military, and economic support for the Nicaraguan revolution, and this directly affected the negotiating capacity of the Sandinista government in the Esquipulas peace process.

On 14 February 1989, at Costa del Sol, El Salvador, only 1 day before the Soviet withdrawal from Afghanistan, the five Central American presidents signed the Tesoro Accord. This accord reopened the difficult process of verification, essential for the success of the peace process. The heads of state also promised "to elaborate, within 90 days, a joint plan for the demobilization, voluntary repatriation or relocation in Nicaragua and in other countries, of members of the Nicaraguan Resistance and their families" (Moreno 1994, p. 203). Meanwhile, Nicaragua announced that an election would be held in February 1990. These resolutions were eventually put into effect by three different groups: the newly created Comisión Internacional de Apoyo y Verificación (CIAV, International Commission of Support and Verification), which would assist in the voluntary demobilization and repatriation or relocation of the Contras; the UN Observer Group in Central America (ONUCA), which would monitor the security commitments of Esquipulas; and the UN Observer Mission for Verification of Elections in Nicaragua, which would monitor the Nicaraguan 1990 election (Baranyi and North 1992).

At this time, the recently elected President of the United States, George Bush, insisted on maintaining the Contras to keep pressure on the Sandinistas. Nevertheless, it was clear by then that the Bush Administration was not as committed as the Reagan one had been to a military solution in Nicaragua. In fact, Bush used the Esquipulas process as an opportunity "to shift from an obsessive and exclusively military focus on Central America to a policy designed for Latin America as a whole, one which would widen Reagan's narrowly geopolitical focus to emphasize more pressing 'geo-economic' issues: debt, drugs, and trade" (Envío 1989, p. 5).

The resolutions reached at Costa del Sol were ratified at the Cumbre de Tela meetings on 5–7 August 1989. The results of this meeting were important because they represented significant progress on the details and implementation of the Esquipulas peace process, including the disarming and dismantling of the Contras and the establishment of dates and conditions for the Nicaraguan elections. In this sense, Cumbre de Tela's most important achievement was the activation of both ONUCA and CIAV (Tinoco 1988).

Why did the Esquipulas process succeed? To answer this question, one must consider both the role of political agency and the changing international conditions under which the process took place.

In Nicaragua, perestroika and glasnost represented not only a major blow to the anti-imperialism of the FSLN but also a legitimization of liberal-democratic politics, criticized and condemned by the FSLN. Furthermore, the events in the Soviet Union reduced Managua's economic capacity to sustain its war effort. By 1989, the gross domestic product per capita had fallen to 42% of its 1977 level; the total export value, to 53%; and real wages, to 24%. Moreover, Nicaragua's accumulated foreign debt per capita was the highest in Latin America: US $3 000, or 33 times the value of export goods (GON 1992). And the poor economic conditions were aggravated by the social wounds resulting from the war. According to Oquist (1992, p. 7),

> *The 61,884 victims of war represent 1.72 percent of the Nicaraguan population of 3.6 million inhabitants. The 30,865 deaths represent 0.86 percent of the population. The same percentage of the U.S. population of 250 million would be 2,125,000 deaths, a figure almost equal to all the Americans killed in action and dead from other causes in all the wars in U.S. history.*

The increasingly embarrassing illegality of US support for the Contras, along with the Contras' inability to achieve significant political or military victories, encouraged Washington to find another solution to "the Nicaraguan problem." More important, however, was the end of the Cold War, which compelled the United States to shift its foreign-policy priorities away from anticommunist crusades in Central America and to place more emphasis on political methods to displace the Sandinistas. As Robinson and MacMichael (1990, p. 32) pointed out, "the slogan in Washington changed from 'support the freedom fighters' to 'democratization in Nicaragua'." Washington's new strategy coincided with the Esquipulas peace process, which focused on the use of elections to achieve peace in the region. In this context, the Sandinistas scheduled the national election for February 1990. As Peter Rodman, a National Security Council representative, stated in his testimony to the Bipartisan Commission on Free and Fair Elections in Nicaragua, Washington saw this election as an opportunity "to test the Nicaraguans, to mobilize all international pressure possible against [the Sandinistas] ... to transfer the conflict in Nicaragua to the political terrain" (Robinson and MacMichael 1990, p. 32).

The United States provided technical and financial support for the Nicaraguan opposition coalition, the Union Nacional de Oposición (national opposition union), and continued to put military and economic pressure on the Sandinistas. From 1989 to 1990, the US Congress paid US $12.5 million to try to influence the Nicaraguan political process (Robinson and MacMichael 1990). If a similar calculation is made for the 5-year period before the February 1990 election, "the covert and overt support to Anti-Sandinista political groups in Nicaragua," according to Hemisphere Initiatives, "totalled $26.1 million" (Fine et al. 1990, p. 35). Cortés Dominguez (1990) calculated that the external support for the anti-Sandinista opposition between 1984 and 1989, including funding from sources other than the United States, was US $29.6 million.

The softening of the positions of both the US government and the Sandinistas created better conditions for achieving peace. The success of the Esquipulas process was based on the ability of its promoters to exploit the new opportunities opened by the weakening of both Managua and Washington. The weakening of these two adversaries facilitated the deactivation of destructive political trends and helped create new opportunities for a political negotiation of the crisis.

The nature of the peace achieved

The end of the Cold War created new historical conditions that induced Nicaraguan domestic contenders and the US government to put an end to the Contra War. From this perspective, the most important contribution of the mission for peace in Nicaragua was to take advantage of the opportunities presented by new relations between East and West to create the historical conditions for Nicaraguan political actors to construct a minimum social consensus as the foundation of social order and peace.

However, the articulation of this consensus was a difficult task in a country that achieved peace as a result of predominantly external circumstances that forced power contenders to stop killing each other. The peace achieved in Nicaragua was not the result of an autonomous domestic process of negotiation and compromise among the primary Nicaraguan power contenders. It was not a process whereby power contenders reached some fundamental agreements regarding the organization of the social, political, and economic life of the country. Peace in Nicaragua was simply a stop to the war, forced by external conditions that made it impossible for the Sandinistas and the Contras to continue their military confrontation. The success of the mission for peace in Nicaragua was not based on its capacity to bring the power contenders to an agreement about the future of the country; rather, the mission for peace succeeded because of its capacity to use the opportunities created by the end of the Cold War to officialize an *alto al fuego* (cease-fire).

This is not to deny the value and significance of the specific terms and conditions of the peace agreement, especially those concerning the organization of national elections. However, the international conditions under which the peace process took place made these terms and conditions almost inevitable. The mission for peace in Nicaragua simply facilitated the identification of the modality and process whereby Nicaraguans would comply with the requirements of the emergent new world order. These requirements included the dismantling of the centrally planned economy and the political structures established by the Sandinistas and their replacement with a free-market economy and a democratic electoral system. In this framework of historical limitations and opportunities, Nicaraguans now have to articulate a minimum social consensus that can create the conditions for durable peace.

In other words, the normative framework for the consolidation of peace in Nicaragua is the result of external pressures, rather than being the product of a domestic process of negotiation and compromise (to talk about a normative framework is to talk about a set of premises, principles, and priorities that determine the nature of relations between the state, economy, and society that one wishes to attain). From this perspective, electoral democracy in Nicaragua gives people the capacity to choose the governments in charge of administering states that function predominantly in accordance with the principles and requirements of the international economic system as expressed by the policies of the international organizations making up the "Washington consensus." Democracy does not offer the Nicaraguan people the opportunity to condition and determine the functions and priorities of the state. This situation may widen the traditional gap between state and society in Nicaragua and intensify the unresolved social tensions and contradictions that have plagued Nicaraguan society.

The separation of the Nicaraguan state from its society and its increasing dependence on external forces reduces the possibility of using state power as an effective instrument for the articulation of a social consensus on the future of Nicaraguan society. Without the state as a central point of reference for political participation and competition, the object of political conflict in Nicaragua may be displaced onto civil society and reoriented outside established political processes and institutions. The deinstitutionalization of conflict in Nicaragua may intensify political fragmentation and create conditions for a "war of all against all." Evidence of this fragmentation can be found in the crisis of governability, the low levels of legitimacy enjoyed by the state (see Delgado Romero 1995; IEN 1995), and the unprecedented levels of suicide and criminal activity in both urban and rural areas of the country. According to statistical information compiled by the Ministry of Health, the proportion of violent deaths by suicide went from 6.02% in 1992 to 6.95% in 1993, to 8.08% in 1994, and to 10.10% in 1995 (El Semanario 1996). (For the problem of crime and security in Nicaragua, see Cuadra Lira [1997].) Further evidence can be found in the persistence, in the north-central region, of armed groups that continuously challenge the authority of the state. The growing levels of poverty and social inequality are also indications of fragmentation in Nicaragua: it has been estimated that 37% of the Nicaraguan population suffers from "extreme poverty"; 30%, from "poverty" (see Martinez Vega and Ghysels 1995). Other indications are the serious cultural divisions created by the Nicaraguan diaspora; the return to Nicaragua of thousands of exiles after the elections of the 1990; and the tendency toward the politicization of religious loyalties, as expressed in the formation of evangelical political parties and the increasing political influence of the Roman Catholic Church.

Did the Peace Process Fail? Lessons for Canada

The above analysis might lead one to conclude that the Central American peace process has failed in Nicaragua. This conclusion is valid only if one assumes that missions for peace are designed to eliminate conflict. I argue that the most a mission for peace can achieve in a country like Nicaragua is the deactivation of destructive historical forces and their temporary reorientation toward manageable levels. This is no minor accomplishment. Missions for peace can create new opportunities that the elites of politically polarized and socially divided societies can use to construct a stable social consensus. At minimum, this consensus "must include agreements regarding the permanent rules governing the competition for public office; the resolution of conflict; the reproduction of capital; and the appropriate role of the state, particularly the military and the bureaucracy" (Karl 1986, p. 10).

The limited expectations of the effectiveness of missions for peace expressed here should not be interpreted as a fatalistic assessment of the capacity of political will to shape history. The existence of structural limitations does not prevent political activity from deactivating, or even reversing, historical trends. However, to assume that missions for peace can by themselves solve the historical tensions and contradictions that generate violent conflict in countries like Nicaragua is to fall victim to a voluntaristic understanding of social conflict in which human will, political decision, and legal accords are considered the most important determining factors in the shaping of history.

Canada played a useful and important role in the Central American peace process. At the technical level, Canada contributed to the difficult and crucial task of verifying the security commitments of the Contadora and Esquipulas processes. At the political level, Canada participated in an international coalition that provided political support for the search for peace in Central America. By operating at these two levels, Canada not only supported the implementation of the Contadora and Esquipulas processes but also helped to expand the political space within which these initiatives evolved. Canada contributed to the creation of a new political space for the Central American peace process by actively promoting an interpretation of the sources, nature, and implications of the Central American crisis that was significantly different from that of the United States. Whereas Washington considered the Central American conflict a product of East–West tensions, Ottawa felt that the crisis was the result of domestic social conditions (see YCISS 1986). In 1988, the first report of the House of Commons Special Committee on the Peace Process in Central America indicated that "the root causes of conflict in the region are mass poverty and recurrent cycles of economic collapse" (GOC 1988, p. 21). According to this multidimensional view of the roots of the Central American crisis (GOC 1988, p. 3),

> *The region has been beset by multiple conflicts for many years. Factionalism and the power of the military have impeded the*

development of civil governments, and, indeed have made them impossible in some countries for long periods of time. Disputes between states have poisoned the atmosphere throughout Central America. Intertwined has been a geo-political dimension: the intimate involvement of the superpowers, historically, the United States and more recently the Soviet Union, has immensely complicated attempts at reconciliation.

This interpretation of the roots of the Central American crisis is consistent with those presented in both the report of the Special Joint Committee of the Senate and the House of Commons on Canada's International Relations in 1986 (GOC 1986) and that of the Sub-committee on Canada's Relations with Latin America and the Caribbean in 1982 (GOC 1982).

The report of the Special Joint Committee on Canada's International Relations argued that "human rights violations in Central America arise from the failure of economic development, the frequent absence of political alternatives to dictatorships and military regimes, social upheaval, increasing cycles of violence, and external intervention" (GOC 1986, p. 111). The final report of the Sub-committee on Canada's Relations with Latin America and the Caribbean pointed out that (GOC 1982)

The mounting violence in Central America, which is threatening to engulf the entire region, arises primarily from internal causes. It is however, reinforced and spread by the injection of outside ideological concerns and by the provision of military assistance to both repressive governments and revolutionary groups.

By contributing to the technical implementation of the peace process and by creating new political space for peace negotiations, Canada supported "the solution of internal political, economic and social problems by the countries and peoples of the region themselves" (Charland 1984, p. 4).

Rather than expanding the role of missions for peace to include the highly desirable but impractical objective of peacebuilding, Canada should explore ways to develop its political capacity to support the creation of opportunities for negotiation and compromise among power contenders in polarized societies. This is because the complete transformation of the social structures responsible for violent conflict lies beyond the legal, political, and institutional capacity of missions for peace.

A neutral forum for continuous dialogue among the affected country's political contenders can be very helpful for the continued success of a peace accord. Canada can provide such a forum through institutions such as the International Centre for Human Rights and Democratic Development. This dialogue should not be considered a substitute for the domestic political process essential for the consolidation of peace. The value of a neutral forum provided by Canada would be in enabling participants to receive information and analyses that help them identify the conditions that limit their political choices and strategies. It would be an opportunity for power contenders to avoid the narrow focus and intensity of the political discussions that always accompany the aftermath of peace negotiations. Such discussions obscure the structural conditions within which political competition takes place. They reduce politics to a competition for power and to a clash of wills that can easily degenerate into violence. By clarifying the structural conditions, an organized neutral dialogue can help identify points of convergence and common ground among power contenders. Such assistance would be compatible with Canada's noninterventionist position in the Third World, limited finances for participation in the promotion of global peace, and solid international reputation for fairness and impartiality.

Needless to say, dialogue for the stabilization of peace in Nicaragua or any other polarized society involves the risk of failure. In the final analysis, all that missions for peace can do is to facilitate the creation of opportunities within which members of a polarized society can reach a social consensus as a foundation for a durable peace. A realistic approach to missions for peace must face the fact that no amount of political support or financial aid can prevent a country from destroying itself.

Conclusions

Missions for peace should not be conceived of as a form of intervention designed to solve the social, political, and economic problems of a troubled society. The most that they can hope to achieve is the deactivation of destructive historical forces and their temporary reorientation toward more manageable levels. By doing this, missions for peace can create new historical opportunities that the elites of politically polarized and socially divided societies can use to begin to construct a minimum social consensus as the foundation of a durable peace.

The peace process in Nicaragua brought about the end of that country's civil war and prevented the conflict from spreading to neighbouring countries. Although conditions for peace in Nicaragua remain fragile, the prospect of a regional war has all but disappeared. In this context, then, the two most important achievements of the peace process were the deactivation of the historical and structural conditions and trends that from 1979 to 1990 progressively moved toward the regionalization of the war; and the creation of opportunities for the stabilization of peace. The maintenance and protection of these opportunities can be enhanced if Canada involves itself in the organization of a neutral forum for a continuous dialogue among the political factions of the country. This forum would help Nicaraguans identify points of convergence among political rivals that would be useful in recreating the Nicaraguan state.

Chapter 3

Cambodia

Foreign policy and missions for peace

Gérard Hervouët

The overthrow of the Sihanouk regime, in March 1970, started the conflict in Cambodia that brought the unexpected devastation of this small country. The interference of the United States made Cambodia a major focus of regional and international rivalry and intervention. The coup against

NB. The present paper forms part of my ongoing research on Cambodia. It is based on numerous interviews, and it would be impossible to list the names of all those people who generously contributed to the study. However, I would like to express my particular gratitude to the North Asia directorate of the Department of External Affairs in Ottawa and to its former director, Mr Joseph P. Caron, as well as to David Edwards and Leslie James for their helpful comments on the first draft.

Sihanouk was immediately followed by an internal war between the republican regime of Lon Nol and the radical Khmer Rouge communist revolutionary movement, inspired by the cultural revolution in China. The victory of the Khmer Rouge in April 1975 brought a radical transformation of the country, with an enormous human cost, bloody internal purges, and repeated attempts to confront Viet Nam and revive the long-standing ethnic antagonism between the Vietnamese and Khmer peoples.

In December 1978, the Vietnamese army officially launched a campaign against Kampuchea. The operation was carried out swiftly, and it quickly achieved its basic objective, which was to overthrow the Khmer Rouge government. The Heng Samrin government became the surrogate of Viet Nam, to which it was bound by the Treaty of Peace, Friendship and Cooperation of 18 February 1979. This treaty lent legitimacy to the presence of the Vietnamese troops and incorporated Kampuchea into the so-called Fédération indochinoise (Indochinese federation) that Viet Nam, supported by Laos, has long been suspected of promoting. The Heng Samrin regime was then completely subservient to the Vietnamese government and had no choice but to collaborate and to place both troops and supplies at its disposal.

After Viet Nam invaded Cambodia in 1978, the conflict became one of the major issues in international relations. China strongly opposed Viet Nam's ambition — an ambition supported by the Soviet Union — to see its allied regime in Phnom Penh emerge as the dominant power in Cambodia. China demonstrated its resoluteness during the Kampuchea conflict by launching a military offensive against Viet Nam in February 1979. The punitive operation failed. China abstained from giving Hanoi a "second lesson" but instead provided a lot of weapons to the Khmer Rouge.

Viet Nam's policies also met opposition from the Association of Southeast Asian Nations (ASEAN), which each year mobilized a very efficient diplomatic coalition in the United Nations to deny legitimacy to Viet Nam's position and Heng Samrin's regime. An ASEAN-sponsored annual resolution condemning Viet Nam's occupation of Cambodia prevented the People's Republic of Kampuchea (PRK) from taking Cambodia's seat at the United Nations (UN). With military supplies from China and from some ASEAN members and with the cooperation of Thailand, the Coalition Government of Democratic Kampuchea (CGDK) was able to mount a guerrilla campaign that prevented the PRK from consolidating its position and for many years put thousands of Vietnamese troops into a costly and unwinnable struggle.

Despite many attempts at mediation in this multilevel conflict, nothing seemed to affect the stalemate. However, by mid-1980, the new Soviet policy and Gorbachev's initiatives to improve Sino–Soviet relations began to open new avenues for settlement. At the end of 1987, when Prince Sihanouk and PRK Premier Hun Sen held discussions, a series of negotiations among the Cambodian parties was initiated. In July 1988, Indonesia, which had since 1984 been trying to moderate ASEAN's tough position toward Viet Nam, hosted informal multilateral talks among the Cambodian parties, along with Viet Nam, Laos, and ASEAN members. Jakarta's informal meetings led to an international conference on Cambodia in Paris at the end of July 1989.

The conference was not a complete success, but it was attended by the four Cambodian factions; the six ASEAN countries; China, France, Russian Federation, United Kingdom, and United States, the five permanent members of the UN Security Council; and Australia, Canada, India, Laos, Viet Nam, and Zimbabwe, representing the nonaligned movement. The conference adopted a general blueprint for peace and a comprehensive settlement concept. In September 1989, Viet Nam announced its withdrawal from Cambodia. After 1 year of intense negotiations, the four Cambodian parties accepted a framework developed by the five permanent members of the Security Council and set up the Supreme National Council (SNC), which would occupy Cambodia's seat at the UN.

The conflict was not yet over, and the Phnom Penh regime continued to express reservations. Only in June and August in Pattaya (Thailand) did the four parties agree on a cease-fire, the cessation of foreign military assistance, and the various clauses of UN mechanism to be implemented by the UN Transitional Authority in Cambodia (UNTAC). These two Pattaya agreements paved the way for the formal Paris Conference and the transitional phase, which began on October 1991. Once again, Canada was to play a role in one of the most important peace operations of the UN.

Canada and Indochina: the Historical Landmarks

In seeking to understand Canada's role, it is essential to remember that Canada's early involvement with Southeast Asia, particularly with Indochina, took place in the context of the International Commissions for Control and Supervision (ICCSs) in Cambodia, Laos, and Viet Nam. Such a reminder is necessary, given that the Indochinese experience profoundly marked the collective memory of Canadian diplomacy. Canada was twice invited to participate in these missions, first in 1954, at the conclusion of the Geneva Conference, and on a second occasion in the fall of 1972, when a cease-fire agreement appeared possible in Viet Nam.

In 1972, Canada learned, without any enthusiasm, that the Democratic Republic of Viet Nam and the United States had agreed to create a new ICCS, comprising Hungary, Indonesia, Poland, and, once again, Canada. Failure to achieve a cease-fire agreement in October allowed Ottawa, which happened to be in the middle of an election campaign, to postpone a decision on whether to participate in the ICCS. However, an accord was signed on 27 January, and, as expected, Canada was called on to join the commission, alongside the three other participating nations.

Ottawa again found itself in a role it had not particularly coveted. Constrained by events, Canada was unwilling to assume responsibility for the reopening of the fragile accord if it refused to participate; nor was it in a position to turn down a role that was the logical outgrowth of its oft-repeated wishes to see the United States withdraw from Viet Nam. The United States, which was trying hard to extricate itself from Viet Nam, also wanted Canadian expertise and experience on the new commission — the United States hoped the ICCS would make the US exit more orderly. China, too, was assuredly favourable to Canadian participation, as it had been in 1954. In the context of Sino–Canadian rapprochement and the trade negotiations then under way between Ottawa and Beijing, Canada would have had a delicate time ducking a Chinese request. With considerable caution, Canada committed itself for an initial period of 60 days and sent a contingent of 290 military and civilian personnel to Viet Nam. In February 1973, Ottawa recognized the government of the Democratic Republic of Viet Nam, a move "equivalent to effectively according legal status to the governments of the two Vietnams" that should have "facilitate[d] the task of the Canadian delegation to the ICCS" (Sharp 1973, p. 19).

The following month, the Secretary of State for External Affairs traveled to Indochina, where he met with authorities of the Hanoi, Saigon, and Vientiane governments. Appearing before the Commons Standing Committee on External Affairs and Defence after his return, Mitchell Sharp reported that, despite the considerable efforts made by the Canadian delegation, the ICCS had been unable to accomplish the tasks it had been assigned at the conclusion of the cease-fire agreement. There had been thousands of incidents, several of them large-scale operations. However, for a Canadian withdrawal not to unduly undermine the fragile structure of peace in Viet Nam, the government decided to prolong Canadian participation in the ICCS for another 60 days. At the end of this new delay, on 29 May 1973, Sharp announced Canada's withdrawal from the commission, effective 31 July 1973.

The events of 1975 in Indochina had relatively little influence on the Canadian position. When the Khmer Rouge captured Phnom Penh on 17 April, overthrowing the Lon Nol regime, Canada recognized the new government of Kampuchea without having to establish diplomatic relations. On 25 June 1975, not long after the evacuation of Canadian Embassy personnel from Saigon, Canada established new diplomatic ties with the provisional government of the Republic of South Viet Nam. When the unification of Viet Nam was completed the following year, Canada was not obliged to officially recognize the new state, as its relations were the continuation of those already established with the former governments of North and South Viet Nam. In Laos, the rise to power of the Pathet Lao, in August 1975, did nothing to modify the Canadian attitude. Ottawa simply pursued relations established on 15 June 1974 with the preceding government, and the Canadian ambassador to Thailand retained his accreditation with the government in Vientiane.

Canada might have been expected to react more strongly to the December 1978 Vietnamese invasion of Cambodia. Instead, its response to these events was remarkably discreet; with an equally surprising degree of discretion, Canada put an end to its aid program for Viet Nam in February. The 1979 federal election campaign pushed the Indochinese question well down the list of priorities for ministers and parliamentarians alike. At a Security Council meeting on 24 February 1979, however, the Canadian delegate, in concert with the delegates of Australia and New Zealand, expressed concerns over the Cambodian situation.

The election of a Conservative government in 1979 brought with it a hardening of the Canadian position; the shift was linked to a strategy that focused on human-rights promotion and reinforcement of ties with China and ASEAN but was also favourable to the maintenance of Canadian involvement in the United Nations and multilateral diplomacy. The origins of the first element of this strategy can undoubtedly be traced to the political climate prevailing at that time, as well as to principles defended by the White House. Then Secretary of State for External Affairs, Flora MacDonald, unambiguously declared her intention to ensure that "Canadian foreign policy place[s] even greater emphasis on human rights issues" (MacDonald 1979, p. 2). She added that "we will be on watch for any violations of international agreements such as the Universal Declaration of Human Rights, and the Helsinki Accords." In parallel to this focus on rights, however, the government gave top priority to opening up markets in China and in ASEAN, despite repeated denunciations of certain ASEAN nations (particularly Indonesia and the Philippines) in Amnesty International's annual reports. The inherent paradox went largely unnoticed by the Canadian population.

As mentioned earlier, Canadian aid to Viet Nam was suspended in February 1979. Speaking to the Canadian Club in Montréal, on 17 December, MacDonald (1979) specified that "given the policy of human rights violations recently adopted by Vietnam, we have suspended all aid programs to this country." This speech, like many other public statements, made no reference to Kampuchea. In November, however, the Canadian government had cosponsored UN Resolution A/34/L.13. Presented by the ASEAN nations, it called for an end to hostilities, the withdrawal of all foreign forces from Kampuchea, and the peaceful resolution of differences.

For a long period, Canada supported this resolution while refusing to recognize the Vietnamese-backed Heng Samrin regime in Kampuchea. As a result, Canada found itself, like many other countries, in the embarrassing position of maintaining recognition of the former Khmer Rouge regime as the sole legitimate Kampuchean government, a judicial contortion corrected by the unreserved condemnation of the genocide practiced by the Pol Pot regime. In June 1982, when China and the ASEAN countries joined together to back the formation of a CGDK — consisting of the Khmer Rouge, Prince Sihanouk, and former premier Son Sann — Canada endorsed the proposition to recognize the CGDK as the sole legitimate government in Kampuchea.

In sum, then, Canada maintained identical policies on Indochina during the roughly 10 years ending with the opening of the first Paris Conference on Cambodia in 1989. These policies can be clearly situated within the framework of traditional Canadian adherence to the principles of the UN Charter; Canada's multilateral strategy of solidarity with Western positions; and a certain tendency, despite considerable Canadian reservations, to follow the path charted by US diplomacy.

Without disregarding these constraints, Canada nonetheless began, for economic reasons, to gradually reexamine its attitude toward East Asia and Southeast Asia. This reexamination and the emerging awareness of Asian importance occurred by the late 1970s, particularly in the wake of the second energy crisis in 1979, an event that motivated the Canadian business community to take a closer look at the Pacific Basin. In less then 10 years, the changes brought about by the economic dynamism of the region forced the acknowledgment of new and unavoidable realities. As External Affairs Minister Joe Clark noted in 1989,

> *Today, more than half of our exports destined for countries other than the United States are shipped to the Asia–Pacific Region. They represented more than 17 billion dollars in 1988. Approximately three quarters of our exports to Korea and Japan come from the four Western provinces. The proportion is about 90% for China. Last year, our total Asia–Pacific exports grew by over 30%. Within ten years, the value of bilateral trade between Canada and the region will exceed 50 billion dollars.*
>
> Clark (1989a, p. 1)

Along with trade considerations came a growing awareness of the importance of Asian investment in Canada and the realization that visits to Canada by Asian tourists accounted for 28% of the tourist trade. The fact that Asians constituted the majority of Canadian immigrants only served to drive home the new-found importance of the Pacific Basin to Canadian society. Gradually, the region became a priority, a priority often associated with a certain sentiment of urgency and a need to make up lost ground. Despite this, the federal government continued to manifest its traditional reservations in the regional-security field and was unable to surmount the long-standing reticence born of its earlier interventions in Southeast Asia.

As early as 1972, the Standing Senate Committee on Foreign Affairs had noted the caution, indeed the extreme discretion, of Canada with regard to regional security in Asia and the Pacific. The committee wrote the following: "Pacific countries are anxious to see what role Canada will play in the achievement of regional peace and security and in cooperative action to share the benefits of economic development with the disadvantaged countries" (SSCFA 1972). This remark went unheeded, and in 1986 the Special Joint Committee on the External Relations of Canada concluded that "in security matters, however, military resources do not allow (Canada) to contribute directly to the maintenance of security in this region" (SJCERC 1986). This acknowledgment of Canadian impotence, linked with its participation in the ICCS in Indochina between 1954 and 1973, only hardened Canada's resolve to keep its distance from the region. Furthermore, it was with a certain legitimacy that Ottawa justified the priority status that Canada gave to European defence and to its own role in the North Atlantic Treaty Organization.

Nonetheless, it was becoming increasingly difficult to explain, often within the same documents and speeches, that Asia and the Pacific were henceforth more important economically to Canada than Europe, that Asian immigration exceeded that from European sources, but that the federal government remained firmly committed to its traditionally cautious stance on regional-security matters. Already in 1988, but most notably as of 1989, unprecedented upheaval in the international system was modifying perceptions of Canadian foreign policy. The lessening of tensions in Europe facilitated a more marked shift of interest toward the Pacific. Pressured by events, the federal government in Ottawa also came to understand that Canada's interests would be better served by according greater credibility to Canada's Asian vocation. Along with the need to reinforce its West Coast fleet, the federal government grew conscious of the fact that it could no longer pursue uniquely economic interests within the existing regional forums. To be considered a serious actor, Canada also had to participate in the conferences determining the strategic future of the Asia–Pacific region.

The first test of this still nascent desire to play a role in East Asian security came when Viet Nam invited Canada to join an international peacekeeping body to supervise the withdrawal of Vietnamese troops from Cambodia. The invitation came as no surprise. Canada had known for more than 2 years that Viet Nam would be making such a request when favourable conditions were in place. Ottawa reacted swiftly: on 5 April 1989, the Department of External Affairs issued a press release to decisively underscore Canadian interest in the rapid resolution of the Cambodian question and, by the same token, Southeast Asian stability and security. The Canadian (EAC 1989) response imposed certain conditions but closed no doors:

> *Canada had advised Vietnam that we would only consider participation if key conditions can be met including: the full support of all parties to the dispute, a clear mandate and a limited duration of involvement; manageable resources implications; and, most importantly, evidence that this is part of an effective and comprehensive solution to the Cambodian problem.*

The insistence on an effective, global solution underlined Canada's attachment to, and alignment with, the positions of the ASEAN countries and the CGDK. These positions excluded any partial settlement that would result in the suspension of aid to the Cambodian factions and the withdrawal of Vietnamese troops but leave the internal political situation unresolved.

The diplomatic ballet around the Cambodian question then moved into an accelerated phase as details of a major conference to be attended by the five permanent members of the Security Council took shape. The meeting, which was to be co-chaired by France and Indonesia, was scheduled for 30 July 1989 in Paris. Invitations were sent not only to the five permanent members of the Security Council but also to the ASEAN countries, the four Cambodian factions, Australia, India, and Japan. But Canada's invitation was late in materializing. This delay both worried and embarrassed Ottawa, which felt that its absence from the conference might damage the credibility of its newly expressed interest in Southeast Asia. Thanks to some international lobbying, particularly the intervention of Canada's mission to the United Nations, Canada finally succeeded in obtaining an invitation, which arrived from Paris on 21 July.

This incident clearly illustrated the motivations of the Canadian government and its policies on the Cambodian question. On one hand, it wished to maintain and reaffirm its attachment to UN principles; on the other, it aimed, by way of its involvement in Cambodia, to highlight a renewed foreign-policy interest in Southeast Asia. With regard to the first of these objectives, External Affairs Minister Joe Clark, in a speech in Paris on 30 July (Clark 1989b), made a vibrant plea for eventual UN involvement in the settlement of the Cambodian problem:

> *No other organization commends the same authority in providing guarantees. No other organization has the necessary machinery in place to move quickly to implement agreements once they are reached. No other organization spans as effectively the interlinked security, humanitarian and economic agenda of this conference. We are aware that other options have been proposed, such as the creation of a control commission. In our experience those are highly imperfect instruments, especially if they do not have an appropriate reporting authority or an integrated mission structure.*

In fact, Clark wanted Canada to participate in an international control mechanism (ICM) in Cambodia, and the forum of the Paris Conference allowed him to remind participants of Canadian expertise in the peacekeeping field: "Our earlier experience in Indochina has taught us what will not work; our experience in over 20 peacekeeping operations elsewhere gives us an appreciation of what does make for success" (Clark 1989b). The message was clear: Canada was available but was resolved to have a say in determining the nature of the mechanisms to be put in place.

With regard to the second Canadian objective, Clark insisted, in the same speech, on the emergence of Southeast Asia and added that "it is surely time to associate Indochina as a whole with this remarkable success story and to allow the talents and resources of the Indochina countries to strengthen South East Asian success" (Clark 1989b). As the 1980s drew to a close, it was becoming evident that Canadian interest in a peaceful solution in Cambodia went beyond Khmer borders. Canada's goals were twofold: to increase its participation in ASEAN economic prosperity and simultaneously to position itself in the face of the possible reintegration of Viet Nam into the Southeast Asian economic-expansion zone. The Under-Secretary of State for External Affairs, de Montigny Marchand (1990, p. 7), made it very clear:

> *The region, including … Indochina, will no doubt continue to undergo the remarkable economic expansion that has generally distinguished it over the past decade. If Canada wishes to take advantage of this growth, it must continue to tighten links with its Asian partners* [author's translation].

The first Paris Conference on Cambodia ended in partial failure at the close of August 1989. The conference was no more able to establish an ICM capable of supervising the withdrawal of Vietnamese troops than to define a transition process and electoral procedures acceptable to the four factions. On the other hand, the conference proceedings were not suspended indefinitely but simply adjourned; during the 2-year interval preceding their resumption, the multiple elements of fragile consensus were put into place, along with innumerable compromises involving overlapping layers of local interests, regional conflicts, and international antagonisms.

In the extraordinary flurry of diplomatic activity that led to the Cambodian settlement, the repeated interventions of the five permanent members of the Security Council were decisive. Indeed, the fate of Cambodia and the mechanisms of the largest peacekeeping mission ever deployed by the United Nations became key issues for the emerging post-Cold War international order. The Chinese intervention, notably with regard to the Khmer Rouge, was also capital. Pragmatically speaking, Chinese cooperation was aimed at securing pardon for the Tien An Men Square incident; above all else, however, the Chinese regime was abandoning its ideological militancy in favour of the unbridled pursuit of economic growth. Following UN General Assembly approval of the peace plan drawn up by the permanent five in mid-October 1990, it took another year and numerous adjustments before an international peace treaty for Cambodia could finally be signed in Paris on 23 October 1991.

It fell to Barbara McDougall, the newly appointed Secretary of State for External Affairs, to sign the Paris Peace Accords. She declared that "we envisage participating in both military and civilian peacekeeping units of the United Nations transitional force in Cambodia" (McDougall 1991). Although the tone was cautious, the decision had already been made in Ottawa. Of course, budgetary restrictions, certain reservations on the part of the Department of National Defence, and, most importantly, Canada's already overextended peacekeeping commitments limited its ability to follow up on its ambitions. Nonetheless, Ottawa sent a delegation of military officers and public servants as part of the United Nations Advanced Mission in Cambodia (UNAMIC), with its first representatives reaching Phnom Penh in mid-November 1991. On 2 March 1992, Ottawa added 100 people to the contingent, bringing the total number of military personnel to 215 when UNTAC was deployed on 12 March (DND 1992).

A POLICY OF TAKING POSITION[1]

How should we evaluate Canada's policies on the Cambodian question for the period beginning with the first Paris Conference in August 1989 and ending with the Paris Peace Accords of October 1991?

Canada approached the Cambodian conflict handicapped by the frustrations of past experience but fully determined to carry out its new intentions regarding regional security. The government's strategy consisted of surmounting internal bureaucratic reservations — still strong in the public service — while elaborating policies meant to give Canada a certain degree of credibility in Indochinese affairs. Canada was able to capitalize on the distance it had established from US positions on Indochina while highlighting its past experience in the region, but most particularly its experience with peacekeeping.

Despite the partial failure of the first Paris Conference in its search for a global solution for Cambodia, this conference did give Canada the opportunity to reinvolve itself to some extent in the

---

[1] Most of the information in this section is based on documents that cannot be quoted or on interviews with individuals officially involved in Canadian foreign policy.

complex maze of Southeast Asian security issues. During the conference, the Canadian delegation ran the risk of being marginalized. The risk was all the more real because Canada had to some degree forced an invitation to the meeting and because several participating states had infinitely more precise and partisan objectives than the Canadians. However, by agreeing, with India, to co-chair the first Working Commission on the Establishment of an International Control Mechanism, Canada marked up points with its expertise, and its credibility was heightened by both its relative neutrality and the excellent performance of Canadian Ambassador Sullivan. The presence of Secretary of State for External Affairs Joe Clark at the two plenary sessions of the conference did not go unnoticed. His attendance underlined how seriously Ottawa viewed Southeast Asian security problems and gave the Minister an occasion to reinforce personal ties with his ASEAN counterparts, especially the Indochinese leaders. Clark's presence also allowed him to play a key role in launching a UN reconnaissance mission to Cambodia. Although the UN Secretary-General had initially suggested the idea for the mission, the mission would probably not have been possible without Clark's initiative and the work carried out by the members of the Canadian delegation — particularly vis-à-vis the Chinese delegation.

Participation in the conference also led to the reinforcement of Canadian diplomatic autonomy and a reevaluation of Canada's policy for Indochina. As a result of this reevaluation, Canada sent a mission to Cambodia in October 1989 and readmitted Cambodia, Laos, and Viet Nam to its development-assistance program. Positive perceptions of Canada's role, reinforced by Canadian expertise and a certain distance already established from US policy, allowed Ottawa to propose another UN mission for the beginning of January 1990 and another meeting of the five permanent members of the Security Council. That meeting took place in Paris on 15 and 16 January of the same year. In general terms, the Paris Conference on Cambodia and its mid-term impact served as a trampoline for Canadian initiatives with targets more regional in scope. Canada wished to clearly establish its solidarity with ASEAN, develop closer ties with Viet Nam, and diminish the isolation of China in the wake of events in June 1989.

Even though throughout this period Canada expressed concern for Cambodian refugees and reiterated its support for human rights, it did not seek a more appropriate way to intervene in the complex web of Cambodian politics. In November 1989, Canada moved to support Australian plans to place Cambodia under "trusteeship" until a free election could be held. In January 1990, the Secretary of State for External Affairs told the House (Clark 1990b, p. 3) that

> *in November, the government of Australia proposed the establishment of an interim administration of the United Nations in Cambodia. Canada unreservedly supports this proposition, for it has the merit of avoiding the problem of power sharing between the Cambodian factions by entrusting the United Nations with the responsibility of administering the country during the pre-electoral period.*

Clark's remarks illustrate how Canada had adopted the Australian position as its own. To the extent that Canberra's policy favoured the UN as a structure for intervention, it conformed to the pattern of Canadian interventions in the past. On the other hand, it seems rather surprising that Canada did not seek to formulate a more Canadian attitude. In fact, Canada had no project as such for Cambodia and was uninterested in joining the fiercely competitive ranks of the numerous mediators and other parties who intervened during the conflict. No particularly Canadian analysis was developed regarding the difficult issue of an internal settlement between factions. Canada remained cautious, formulating no particular point of view on questions specifically concerned with internal issues such as the establishment of a quadripartite government, the use of the term *genocide*, the problem of Vietnamese colonists, or the nature of a future Cambodian constitution.

In fact, the federal government in Ottawa had no wish to further its involvement; in the multilateral framework of concerted diplomacy, it had no intention to confuse issues or take the risk of angering either its Australian partner or the ASEAN countries. Moreover, Canada lacked sufficient resources to establish representation in Phnom Penh and Hanoi. Given that the Canadian Embassy in Bangkok covered the whole Indochinese peninsula, it is not surprising that Canadian information came more often than not from foreign sources.

The deployment of the military component of UNTAC began in mid-November 1991 and was preceded by UNAMIC, which involved 250 people, primarily French and Australian. At the beginning of January 1992, the UN Secretary-General named Japanese diplomat Yasushi Akashi to head the operation and Australian General John M. Sanderson as commander-in-chief of the UN forces.

The military aspect of the operation was then supposed to involve close to 16 000 soldiers from 23 countries. Their general objective was the stabilization of the security situation and the creation of a climate of confidence between opposing groups. More specific tasks were divided into four grand categories: control of the withdrawal and maintenance of the withdrawal of foreign forces and weaponry; cease-fire supervision; disarmament; and mine clearance, which was to be carried out by 5 000 Cambodians trained by UNTAC. The most delicate of these tasks proved to be the second, because during its first phase of operations, UNTAC failed to establish a veritable cease-fire on Cambodian territory. However, UNTAC was also forced to recognize the impotence of its attempts to disarm and confine to cantonments the soldiers of the four factions during the second phase of operations, beginning in June 1992.

One of the greatest difficulties faced by the representative of the UN Secretary-General proved to be that of convincing several participating nations to provide sufficient troops to meet the ambitious objectives laid out in the Paris Peace Accords and keep to the mission timetable, with its culmination in the general election set for the end of May 1993.

Although everything seemed to point to Canada's playing a fairly major role in the Cambodian mission, Ottawa's real intentions and response proved to be of much humbler proportions. Akashi proposed that Canada commit at least 1 000 people to UN logistical, engineering, and health units and indicated that in light of Canadian experience the UN was counting on it to play a major supporting role. His disappointment was considerable. Canada announced on 27 February 1992 that it would send 100 people with the advanced mission, UNAMIC. In May 1992, Ottawa specified that the total Canadian commitment to UNTAC would not exceed 225 people, most destined for transport duty, but 30 would be naval personnel, there to ensure a certain degree of surveillance on the Mekong and on the rivers of the Tonle Sap.

The Canadian contingent in Cambodia was unquestionably tiny in relation to the total 22 000-strong UN military force that was finally deployed. Canadian government budgetary considerations go a long way to explaining this situation; Canada's other UN commitments already involved 2 200 Canadian soldiers. Furthermore, in diplomatic terms, Canada let it be known that quality was more important than quantity and that its personnel, unlike those of many other nations, had vast experience with such missions. Finally, Canada may also have made certain trade-offs in terms of its priorities in Cambodia and former Yugoslavia, and deployment of Canadian troops in Cambodia was much too risky militarily and thus too great a political risk as well.

Despite the relative modesty of its military participation, the Canadian contingent acquitted itself admirably in the often difficult and thankless task of transporting the thousands of UN troops arriving at the port of Sihanoukville. The presence of a handful of Canadian officers within the UN command structure also ensured that Canada remained at the heart of military decision-making. In contrast, the absence of a full-time Canadian ambassador in Phnom Penh deprived Canada of a closer association with the political process. Akashi and Sanderson quickly took to consulting the Phnom Penh ambassadors of the Security Council member countries. Organized into an informal contact group — also associated with Germany, Indonesia, Japan, and, on occasion, Thailand — these diplomats not only intervened in meetings of a military nature, but also frequently attended sessions of the SNC in an observer capacity. Not until January 1993 was an officer from External Affairs posted to Phnom Penh. With the Cambodian election just a few months away, Canada needed direct access to information to make decisions during this crucial period.

At the beginning of 1993, the political situation in Cambodia was especially tense. The Khmer Rouge were refusing to participate in the second phase of the UN operation, the disarmament and confinement of the troops of each faction to cantonments. This refusal actually modified the terms of the Paris Peace Accords, given that UNTAC had no mandate to use sanctions to ensure that the terms of the accords were respected. After multiple failed attempts by Japan, Thailand, and the co-chairs of the Paris Conference to convince the Khmer Rouge to keep their word, the Security Council was forced to pass a resolution condemning the rebel faction. The resolution set 31 January 1993 as the deadline for the Khmer Rouge to respect the peace agreement and allow UN troops access to their territory.

It quickly became clear that all efforts to force the Khmer Rouge to comply with UN demands would be in vain. It proved virtually impossible to enforce the embargo on fuel imports and timber and gem exports to and from territory controlled by the Khmer Rouge. Military incidents multiplied as the rebel faction openly defied UN authority. In this context, the decision was made in New York and Phnom Penh to hold the election at any price, even if Khmer Rouge refused to participate and only 80% of Cambodian territory was covered.

In the face of this new situation, Canada clarified its stance and unambiguously condemned the lack of Khmer Rouge cooperation; at the same time, Canada recognized that there could be no true and lasting peace without Khmer Rouge participation. Although Canada admitted that the Khmer Rouge's refusal to cooperate meant that the election was inevitable, even in their absence, Ottawa also expressed concern over the potential prolongation of the UNTAC mandate. The general feeling was that Canada would withdraw from the UN operation in the case of an extension,

Thus, at the beginning of 1993, 213 Canadian soldiers and officers were serving with UNTAC forces, and another 50-odd civilians, mostly UN-recruited volunteers, were working in various sectors of the UNTAC operation, notably to prepare for the election. With the election approaching and the campaign beginning on 7 April 1993, the tension escalated. Not only did the Khmer Rouge refuse to cooperate, but they actually increased their attacks on areas close to towns such as Kompong Thom, Siem Reap, and Sisophon. Thirty people were killed and more than 100 injured in an especially violent attack on a train southeast of Battambang on 5 May. (For more details of the numerous events in the lead-up to the election, see, for example, Frost [1993].)

On 10 April, just a few days after the opening of the campaign, Khieu Samphan, head of the Khmer Rouge delegation to the SNC in Phnom Penh, withdrew from the city, thus portending the possibility of attacks on the capital itself. The faction hammered incessantly at its principal argument that "Vietnamese forces of aggression" continued to occupy Cambodia and that the neutral political environment necessary for an election did not exist.

The Khmer Rouge anti-Vietnamese rhetoric was accompanied by massacres of ethnic Vietnamese residents in rural Cambodia. However, neither Khmer Rouge's incidents and intimidation nor accusations such as those brought by the Front uni national pour un Cambodge indépendant, neutre, pacifique et coopératif (FUNCINPEC, united national front for an independent, neutral, peaceful, and cooperative Cambodia) against the Cambodian People's Party (CPP) could cool the ardour of electoral officers responsible for the registration of voters and accredited political parties. On 15 May, the UN Secretary-General officially announced that more than 4.5 million voters (96% of the potential electorate) had been registered. Twenty official parties participated in the election campaign. Although occasionally marked by serious incidents between the three principal factions, the campaign nonetheless allowed all political tendencies to have free expression. UNTAC radio broadcast 15 h a day, and all parties had access to the airwaves.

From 15 to 23 May, the first day of voting, tension only climbed higher. Khmer Rouge radio repeated the same hateful rhetoric toward the Vietnamese community still in Cambodia, denounced violations of the Paris Peace Accords, and made no secret of the dangers facing anybody willing to risk casting a ballot. At UNTAC headquarters in Phnom Penh, Yasushi Akashi (the representative of the Secretary-General) and

General Sanderson remained optimistic to the end, despite the tension. Their resolve stemmed in large measure from the dangers of postponing the election. Failure to keep to the timetable would mean totally discrediting the UNTAC, as well as implying the withdrawal of many of the nations participating in the operation.

Indeed, under the postponement scenario, the cost of each additional day appeared insurmountable for an operation that had already cost close to US $2 billion. Furthermore, information reaching Phnom Penh from throughout the country indicated that the population was determined to vote, whatever the circumstances. Only the Parti libéral démocratique et bouddhiste (PLDB, Buddhist liberal democratic party) risked proposing postponement, but the party quickly backed down in the face of general hostility toward the suggestion. On the military front, General Sanderson had been arguing repeatedly for several months that the Khmer Rouge lacked the resources to attack the 1 400 polling stations and that their real strength had been consistently overestimated. Others noted that even if, in the worst-case scenario, the Khmer Rouge succeeded in preventing 1 million Khmer from exercising their right to vote, the number of voters would still be close to 4 million.

In the days immediately preceding the election, the majority of Cambodia watchers expressed considerable pessimism. The murder, in unclear circumstances, of a Japanese UN volunteer just days before voting began accentuated concern throughout the UNTAC apparatus. The election process was highly vulnerable; a few well-targeted and highly publicized attacks, even minor ones, would have been sufficient to derail this important UN operation.

In Ottawa, the atmosphere was tense. A special Cambodia Task Force comprising representatives from External Affairs, National Defence, and the Canadian International Development Agency (CIDA) was set up in case the situation called for a rapid decision. Pessimism was also widespread in Canada, but officials at External Affairs seemed more optimistic than their colleagues at National Defence. What were the Canadian government's fears? Of primary concern was the safety of the Canadians then in Cambodia. Along with military personnel, some 130 civilians were working for different branches of the UNTAC organization; a further 48 volunteer UN International Polling Station Officers arrived as the elections drew near. Guaranteeing security for the polling-station officers was impossible, given the difficulty of their work and their scattered postings in several Cambodian provinces. Second, Canada feared having to make a decision to withdraw its personnel, which would send a first signal of postponement or cancellation of the elections. A decision to withdraw would have struck a serious blow to UN credibility and threatened all the gains made during the Cambodian operation. Third, Canada feared that the freedom and fairness of the elections would be called into question, creating controversy and yielding results unacceptable to Cambodian political parties. This scenario, too, had its share of potential dangers if, as a result, open conflict broke out between party supporters from the different factions.

From the moment the polls opened on 23 May 1993, early indications rather surprisingly showed that Cambodians were rushing to vote. By the end of the third day of polling, 70% of voters had already cast ballots. The enthusiasm of the population was on occasion hard to contain. In Takeo, Canadians reported that Cambodians had broken down the doors of the polling station to speed the process; elsewhere, such as in Kampong Speu, voters climbed through windows to be the first to cast ballots. Everywhere, long lines formed as Cambodians patiently awaited their turn beneath a premature monsoon rain. In several provinces, Khmer Rouge soldiers voted with their families; 200 participated in Banteay Meanchey province alone. In all, close to 90% of the registered electors voted, a figure well exceeding all expectations.

The most important surprise of the election was the Khmer Rouge decision to radically modify tactics during the final days and hours leading up to the vote, abandoning their plans for sabotage and intimidation. The number of violent incidents in all provinces remained abnormally low in comparison with cease-fire violations recorded during previous periods. However, several difficulties, including minor aggressions and mortar fire, were reported near Khmer Rouge-controlled areas.

After the count, lasting several days because of the difficulty of bringing ballot boxes in from remote areas, FUNCINPEC, with 45.47% of the votes cast, was declared victorious. The CPP took 38.23%; the PLDB placed a distant third, with 3.81%; and the remainder of the votes were split between the 17 other political parties (see Lechervy 1993). On 2 June 1993, Barbara McDougall declared, in a press release, "that the polling phase of the election was free and fair" (McDougall 1993). At the same time, the Minister (McDougall 1993) took the occasion to highlight

> *the role played by some 100 Canadian civilians and over 200 Canadian military personnel in the election process. This has included difficult and sometimes dangerous work over many months by some*

> *35 United Nations volunteers from Canada who helped organize the vote and 50 Canadian polling station officers who supervised balloting and assisted in the count.*

Among the many and diverse civilian components of the UN mission in Cambodia, the electoral component proved to be a grand success. Professor Reginald Austin of Zimbabwe, who had extensive experience in this field, piloted all phases of the electoral operation with unyielding determination and confidence. After the electoral law was adopted by the SNC on 10 January 1992, the registration of political parties, but more particularly of voters, began with remarkable efficiency. By 31 January 1993, more than 4.6 million people were already registered; 800 Cambodian electoral teams assisted by 400 foreign volunteers worked unceasingly to obtain these results. Thirty Canadians recruited by World University Services of Canada joined the election organizers in June 1992. Earlier, in October and November of 1991, a mission coordinated by Ron Gould of Elections Canada had also collaborated in establishing the electoral process.

Another form of Canadian aid was recovery assistance to Cambodia. On 25 January 1990, Joe Clark announced the renewed eligibility of the three Indochinese nations — Cambodia, Laos, and Viet Nam — for Canadian-government development aid. Clark (1990a) referred quite clearly to Cambodia when he asserted the following:

> *We will not have Canadian aid channelled into the military effort of any group. Nor will we permit it to be used by groups or governments whose records demonstrate a fundamental disrespect for basic human rights. We will, for example, insist that no Canadian aid be distributed in areas controlled by the Khmer Rouge.*

A program was officially established in 1991 to finance human-resource development, particularly in the agricultural field in the province of Pursat, through the intermediary of a CIDA-funded consortium of 15 Canadian nongovernmental organizations (NGOs). To this 7-year program's $8.3 million budget should be added the $200 000 contributed annually by the Canadian Embassy in Bangkok. Finally, Canada also contributed $25 000 to the UNTAC human-rights division and an identical amount to the Cambodian Mine Action Centre (CMAC). Although Canadian military involvement in UNTAC officially ended in November 1993, Canada continued to work with CMAC and sent 12 mine-clearance specialists to participate in the centre's operations. Canada's engagement was scheduled to end in February 1996.

Success by default

Whatever the criticisms of the UN operation in Cambodia, in the final analysis, the electoral component was an unexpected success. Running contrary to the rather chaotic trajectories of the other components of the operation, this fundamental success has yet to be definitively explained. It is clear, however, that the electoral process served as a beacon for the mission, which, like a ship buffeted by stormy seas and crosswinds, was taking on water from all sides. Winning the election was a gamble that eventually paid off. However, in the last days of May 1993, the UN operation was in a zero-sum situation; a less fortunate outcome would have forced the international community either to abandon ship or to up the stakes at immeasurable expense.

Numerous evaluations of the operation have been carried out (see, for example, Acharya, [1994] and Amer [1993]; for a perspective on the cultural dimensions, see the interesting piece by Lizée [1993].) Organized generally on a component-by-component basis, these assessments of success and failure are made according to a scale on which the election represents the most positive aspect of the mission; the military intervention, the most negative. In summarizing the essentials, then, without reviewing all the arguments, we could say that the UN admittedly failed to establish a politically neutral climate in Cambodia but nonetheless succeeded in forcing the peripheral actors to soften their positions (Akashi 1993).

Despite the lack of historical distance, it is worth restating the complexity of the external environment, both regional and international. This delayed the elaboration of any solution or intervention in Cambodia. China's decision to rally behind the Security Council, rendered inevitable as it was by circumstances, was undoubtedly the decisive turning point. The gradual withdrawal of Viet Nam, a key actor for so many years, and the decision by the ASEAN countries to conciliate their divergent interests so as to maintain an indispensable united front on the Cambodian question were also essential. In the final analysis, all regional actors came to the realization that permanent instability in Cambodia ran counter to their priorities, which centred on economic growth, development, and the necessary maintenance of the status quo with regard to regional tensions.

It was, of course, difficult to arrive at such fragile consensus on the periphery of the conflict without attempting to deal with the internal sources of Cambodian division. Thus, UNTAC was given the mandate of establishing a politically neutral climate in Cambodia. To make this objective feasible, it was important that the UN more or less take charge of all aspects of the internal conflict and all important dimensions of Cambodian society. The unheralded complexity of the task, a lack of planning, and the large number of countries involved led to improvisation and considerable confusion.

In principle, without legally placing the country under trusteeship, UNTAC was to have acted by virtue of extremely wide-ranging prerogatives in consultation with the SNC, chaired by Prince Sihanouk. In fact, the SNC constituted a sort of legal fiction that enabled UNTAC to take over the administration of a sovereign, UN member state. It goes without saying that the sheer amplitude of the envisaged tasks exceeded by far anything attempted in past operations. The UN, especially the Security Council, found itself in the middle of an operation that went well beyond peacekeeping to encompass an ambitious attempt to re-create, in the space of a short mandate, the political, economic, and social conditions of a society torn by deep-rooted antagonisms ever since the US intervention in the Viet Nam war.

Thus, the three missions, originally conceived of as distinct by UN Secretary-General Boutros-Ghali in the *Agenda for Peace* (Boutros-Ghali 1992), were prematurely telescoped. To the traditional task of peacekeeping was added the task of peacemaking in the field, especially that of peacebuilding. However, as a result of haste and improvisation and, more importantly, in the light of the operational complexities of the 1991 Paris Peace Accords, the huge UN machine was unable to define subtly enough a mission considered as being a test of reconciliation between the five Security Council powers and the numerous regional actors that had been bitterly engaged in the Cambodian conflict for more than two decades. In the rather euphoric post-Paris climate, in which the goodwill of all accord signatories appeared certain, it seemed unimaginable that within a few short months the Khmer Rouge would have broken their promises and, even more surprisingly, refused to yield to the pressures brought to bear by the Chinese government.

Little had been done to set up UNTAC's civilian components. In fact, fewer than 2 000 people were recruited to handle the civilian administration of the country. Only 126 people exercised any real control over the most important ministries in Phnom Penh, that is, those responsible for the administration of 11 000 Cambodian municipalities (Will 1993). It goes without saying that controls were often symbolic, although on occasion very effective.

As early as the spring of 1992, I was able to ascertain that Cambodian authorities (that is, the CPP) harboured considerable scepticism about the UN's capacity to monitor ministerial files and activities. Several considered such an intervention a violation of Cambodian sovereignty; some viewed it as political espionage undertaken on behalf of the other factions to increase their chances of election victory; others simply awaited the arrival of the UN "experts" with a certain cynical amusement, well aware that only a handful would be able to read and speak Khmer (interviews conducted by the author in Phnom Penh in May 1992).

In reality, the vast majority of people recruited by the UN had neither previous experience in Cambodia nor anything but a rudimentary knowledge of Cambodian culture. Even more serious was the fact that many did not even possess the professional expertise required to carry out their duties in the field. As Akashi (1993, p. 189) pointed out, "of the 14 countries that sent over 100 police monitors, 13 were developing countries. Some of the personnel did not meet the highest professional standards." According to several other accounts, it was in Cambodia that these same officers often learned the elementary functions of and role played by a police force in "civil society." Added to this were the communication and comprehension difficulties between UN personnel themselves.

All these criticisms are well documented (for a highly critical account of the entire UN approach to the Cambodian intervention, see Jennar [1995]). Would it have been possible to limit the negative effects of such extensive cultural confusion? This is far from evident in a situation in which the objective was the hasty reconstruction of a society whose social tissues had been severely damaged and degraded; on the other hand, the Cambodian experience, rich in diversity and multiple challenges and exemplary in sheer scope of ambition, offers lessons for future operations responding to similar situations.

The most evident lesson to emerge is the need for the UN to find the means and resources for rapid action. Five long months elapsed between the signing of the Paris Peace Accords and the deployment of UNTAC. Only UNAMIC, with its limited personnel, occupied the terrain, improvising as best it could to lay the groundwork for the larger UN mission. The UNAMIC interlude gave rise to severe criticism, as well as rivalry between French and Australian troops, but was most notable for the hopes it aroused in the Cambodian people, deeply impressed as they were by the determination and unaffected candour of the UNAMIC commander, General Loridon. Eventually, however, UN indecisiveness and sluggishness left much of the population profoundly disillusioned with UNTAC.

The second lesson, linked to the first, arises out of the lack of preparation and the inadequacy of the UN General Secretariat as mission headquarters. As had been the case during other operations, it proved to be very difficult to communicate directly with New York during the Cambodian intervention, or, as an observer put it, UN headquarters did not even maintain a round-the-clock operations room to keep in contact with its field commanders. In the words of Commander-in-Chief General Sanderson (1994, p. 4),

> *In a sense the force Commander has no higher headquarters, and therefore, nobody to talk to about his problems and plans. Of equal concern is the fact that there is no one there who can adequately brief the contributing countries on changes in the operational setting and plans. I had a full realization of this in March 1993 and fortunately was able to prevail upon the Under Secretary General to allow me to establish two UNTAC liaison officers in New York for the purpose of telling everyone what was going on in Cambodia, and telling me what was going on in New York. This was a big improvement.*

All peacekeeping operations face similar challenges: difficulties of preparation, problems of coordination, and the complex task of integrating highly diverse national contingents under a unified command. What was rather new, above and beyond the considerations of a strictly military and technical order, was the introduction of civilian components with a mission more akin to peacebuilding. The Cambodian example clearly revealed the difficulties inherent in this approach. Along with the general unpreparedness characteristic of the Cambodian operation, the incapacity to strategically integrate the work carried out by the seven mission components proved to be another major weakness. Again, Sanderson (1994, p. 11) was clear when he said,

> *To my regret there was never integrated strategic planning within the UNTAC mission. From the very beginning each component conducted a separate survey mission and prepared a plan of sorts. Some component heads were not even appointed before the deployment commenced. Unfortunately, this planning shortfall was never corrected in Cambodia, except in the case of the military and electoral components which forged a necessary planning and control alliance to see the election through.*

Sanderson's criticism is a major one, as it clearly points to problems raised in the case of specific operations by the classic dilemma of cooperation between military and civilian elements. Paradoxically, such cooperation is often more difficult to obtain than dialogue between either element and its counterpart in the country of intervention. Sanderson (1994) also commented on this issue:

> *The reluctance of some civilians to work with the military in an integrated environment is an established fact with missions. It is not simply the linguistic and cultural barriers that have to be broken down, but sociological ones as well. UN civilians are generally individuals rather than team members. Very few of them have any leadership training, and not many have previous experience working with the military. Some, particularly those coming straight out of academia have a positive aversion to the military.*

It goes without saying that if General Sanderson's statements are true, numerous civilians would contend that military personnel also have considerable difficulty working with civilians. Although it is unnecessary to pursue this debate in depth here, it does clearly reveal the need to rethink UN strategies of intervention so as to tie operational tasks more closely to the mission's goals. In the elaboration of such strategies and of the necessary variations meant to accommodate regional and national differences in countries of intervention, it is vital to accord a more important role to NGOs already present in the field, not only by recognizing their greater field experience but also by integrating them, where appropriate, into UN mission components. In the Cambodian case, examples of cooperation were numerous, but examples of integration or even of attempts at concerted action in operating horizontal communications among UNTAC components were rare.

In sketching out what may still be a premature evaluation of Canada's role in Cambodia, it is essential to distinguish two periods: one covering the years between the Vietnamese intervention in Cambodia and the 1989 Paris Conference; and a second one covering the period during which Canada participated in UNTAC.

The first period was marked by Canadian condemnation of Vietnamese intervention, expressed in Canada's annual support for the UN resolution demanding the withdrawal of foreign troops from Cambodia. Although Canada unambiguously condemned the Pol Pot regime, it nonetheless extended diplomatic recognition to the Khmer Rouge as the sole legitimate Cambodian government and supported the coalition government-in-exile, of which the communist faction formed the central element. Canada — alongside the ASEAN nations, China, and the United States — maintained a hard line toward the government in Hanoi so as to force the evacuation of Vietnamese troops from Kampuchea.

Above and beyond the merits of this objective, questions remain about Canadian intransigence toward Viet Nam, a position resembling that adopted toward China during the 1950s and 1960s. In fact, the answers are relatively simple: Canadian foreign policy with regard to Indochina adhered closely to traditions of multilateral diplomacy, the strict respect for Canadian commitments to its traditional allies, and fundamental reservations about involvement in East Asian security matters. During this period, Canada was also reluctant to offend either the ASEAN states or China, nations of central importance to its commercial strategy in Asia. Thus, until the Paris Conference in 1989, Canadian policy on Indochina, and particularly on the Cambodian imbroglio, lacked the kind of initiatives, or even declarations, that would have led observers to conclude that Ottawa had interests in the region other than those related to the humanitarian concerns of the Canadian population toward the boat people.

In other words, Canada followed in the wake of a coalition, without feeling the need to formulate its own analyses or courses of action. Was such caution justified? And did it produce acceptable dividends in the end? Nothing is less certain, given that no particular country in the region insisted that Canada adopt such an intransigent and inflexible code of conduct. On the contrary, my opinion is that if Ottawa had played a more active role in searching for a solution both to the Cambodian conflict and to other regional-security issues, Canada's credibility would have grown in a manner more coherent with the new foreign-policy priority it accorded the Asian region. Why, for example, did Canada abstain during this period from supporting Prince Sihanouk's effort to find an acceptable resolution to the Cambodian problem through dialogue between the Khmer factions? It is, of course, always possible to vaunt the merits of this sort of recommendation after the fact; however, I was already recommending this course of action, among others, in 1988 (Hervouët 1988).

In fact, some Canadian decision-makers thought that too many countries were already engaged in trying to reach a solution. They were convinced that any Canadian proposal would complicate an already highly complex process. However, I still think that Canada was, at that time, too shy. My information and interviews indicated that most Asian countries would have welcomed a greater involvement of Canada, which was regarded with considerable respect and as being the only country able to advance neutral proposals.

Canada's participation in the first Paris Conference on Cambodia in 1989 marked the debut of a process of reflection on the role Canada might play in regional-security matters. Canada discovered at that point that its image and credibility were very good but that the expectations of a Canadian intervention in Cambodia would be commensurately high. According to Job and Langdon (1993, p. 289), virtually all nations participating at the conference recognized and still perceived Canada

> *as having particular expertise and resources relevant to the Asian scene — in peace keeping, verification, surveillance, monitoring and associated confidence-reinforcing technologies — in the organization, design and delivery of development assistance programs.*

Canadian participation in the UN operation in Cambodia was thus something more than its habitual contribution to a peacekeeping mission. It was a test, a test of the desire clearly expressed by External Affairs Minister Joe Clark at the beginning of the 1990s to see Canada take initiatives in Asian security.

In a speech entitled "Canada and Asia Pacific in the 1990s," delivered before the Victoria Chamber of Commerce in July 1990, the Minister took Canadian policy on Asia and the Pacific beyond its traditional trajectory in one sweep, declaring that "our ties to the Pacific go well beyond trade and investment ... the problems of the Pacific are not Pacific problems; they are Canadian. Prosperity in the Pacific is prosperity for Canada. And security in the Pacific is Canadian security" (Clark 1990a, p. 2). With those few words much had changed, even though nothing suggested that Canada had the military resources to become any more involved in regional security than it already was. In fact, the essential message of the speech, repeated in Jakarta, Tokyo, and finally before the UN General Assembly, lay in Clark's intention to establish a Northeast Asian security dialogue.

Christened the Canadian Initiative for a North Pacific Cooperative Security Dialogue, "the basic thrust of this initiative was to assert a more visible Canadian presence in the region ... commensurate with its political and economic interest and its proven multilateral capabilities" (Job and Langdon 1993, p. 289). The proposed initiative provoked a variety of reactions, particularly in Japan and the United States, which were content to maintain bilateral diplomatic initiatives in security matters. Furthermore, by focusing on Northeast Asia, the initiative would exclude Southeast Asia, an exclusion poorly viewed by ASEAN, which "initially viewed the Canadian proposal as an unwelcome, out-of-region initiative" (Henderson 1992/93, p. 114). It would seem curious that the Canadian proposal excluded a zone in which Canada was on the verge of deploying its troops.

Indeed, initiatives and active diplomacy in Northeast Asia coexisted and contrasted strangely with a military intervention in Southeast Asia that was accompanied, paradoxically enough, by a greater degree of diplomatic passivity. This observation could be the subject of another long analysis. Suffice it to say that, henceforth, the Canadian initiative better dovetailed with the interface between the two East Asian subregions. Nevertheless, the fact remains that Canada did not take full advantage of the opportunities provided by the Cambodian situation to prove even further its intentions of participating in regional-security mechanisms. Despite the effectiveness of its Cambodian presence and the remarkable performance of Canadian personnel in the civilian and military components of UNTAC, Canada remained on the margins of the important decisions, cautious in its initiatives and slow to establish a diplomatic presence in Phnom Penh and Hanoi.

Despite the difficulties the Canadian population has had in coming to appreciate the significance of this new reality, Canada is now unavoidably dependent on the state of regional security in the Pacific Basin. Tying in more closely to East Asian economic structures confers new power on Canada, but also it also brings new responsibilities. Any future intervention may thus prove as complex as a Canadian operation in a hypothetical conflict between two members of the European Community would be. In the future, it will no longer be possible to intervene in the region in the sole interest of being "present" or of ensuring the perpetuation of the Canadian peacekeeping tradition through the "neutral" deployment of military personnel. Canada clearly has multiple interests at stake, and its credibility with regard to security matters is now intimately linked to its economic performance and to the density of the complex and varied relations it maintains with each East Asian state.

Recent developments

Events in July 1997 suddenly put the Cambodian instability back into the limelight. Once again, the Khmer country found itself in a state of dramatic uncertainty, given that the "democratic transplant," sprung from the intervention of the UN in 1993, had not held. The fragile coalition between the FUNCINPEC and the CPP broke down following a coup d'état by Co-Prime Minister Hun Sen. His counterpart,

Prince Norodom Ranariddh, who was out of the country at the time, has remained in exile, as did his father after he was a victim of a coup d'état in 1970.

On 5 and 6 July 1997, the armed forces, the majority of which were faithful to Hun Sen's CPP, seized the capital, Phnom Penh, and nearly all the provinces. Several months before, Prince Ranariddh had managed to obtain the defection of thousands of Khmer Rouge and was ready to conclude, with Khieu Samphan (the faction's new leader), an agreement to put an end to 34 years of guerrilla warfare. According to the periodical *Far Eastern Economic Review* (21 August 1997, pp. 14–15), the Khmer Rouge forces were about to recognize the constitution, dissolve their "provisional government," and integrate their troops into the regular army. This historical agreement apparently provoked a notable purge within the Khmer Rouge, particularly the eviction of Pol Pot — the sinister chief, whose recent images have reopened the deep scars left from his executions.

The coalition, sprung from political will but legitimized by the elections and the National Assembly, also split. To mark his disagreement with the policy for reintegration of the Khmer Rouge, Hun Sen seized the occasion to brutally remove Ranariddh. The instability led to the postponement of Cambodia's admission to ASEAN. The international community has remained attentive and has disapproved of the political breakdown of the democratic process that was thought to have been established, at great cost, under the auspices of the UN.

As I have underlined in this study, the assessment of the UN intervention remains the object of controversy and qualified opinions. The success of the electoral process and the massive turnout of the Cambodian electorate remain the most satisfying elements. One would not question the success or ascribe its fragility to the imposition by the UN of one of the most important elements in a democracy.

One can certainly question, however, the premature or precipitate character of the achievement of the electoral process. And the remaining components anticipated by the UN demonstrated highly mitigated — even negative — results. In fact, after the conclusion of the 1993 election, the international community, particularly the UN, was constrained by respect for the sovereignty of the new Cambodian state from interfering in the rivalries between the CPP and FUNCINPEC.

Showing little respect for the commitments of a legitimate process, the Second Co-Prime Minister Hun Sen recently expressed a wish to occupy Cambodia's seat at the UN while threatening to prevent the UN from supervising the Cambodian election, scheduled for May

1998. Needless to say, the UN must maintain a certain coherence between affirming the success of 1993 and refusing to give in to a kind of blackmail that would underline, once again, that one can lose an election but still regain power by force and a fait accompli.

Chapter 4

SOMALIA

WHEN TWO ANARCHIES MEET

Kenneth D. Bush

In the early and mid-1990s, the phrase "like Somalia and Yugoslavia" was a frequent refrain in both policy and academic circles. The phrase punctuated a wide array of positions and policies — many of which were mutually incompatible. Yet, one commentator cautioned enigmatically that "we should be careful not to learn too much from

NB. A version of this chapter appeared in the Spring 1997 issue of the *Journal of Conflict Studies*. It is republished here with the kind permission of the Centre for Conflict Studies, University of New Brunswick, Fredericton, NB, Canada. I thank Todd Baseden, Kerry Buck, Chris Cushing, Nigel Fisher, and Tracey Goodman for their contributions to this chapter.

Somalia." One is faced with two equally important questions: What lessons should be drawn from the case of Somalia? To what extent can these lessons be applied to other complex humanitarian emergencies? These are the principal questions that underpin this study of Somalia and that confront foreign policymakers trying to make sense of the Somalian conflict. On the one hand, Somalia was initially cast as "the ideal test case" for the leadership of the United Nations (UN) in a new and evolving world order (Hutchinson 1993; Jonah 1993). However, the complexities, particularities, and indeterminate outcome of international intervention make it clear that Somalia cannot be used as a model for the construction of a "new" world order. Indeed, unless the international community can discern and learn the appropriate lessons from its experience in Somalia, the case may serve as a convenient justification for retrenchment, isolationism, and retreat from the most pressing challenges of the post-Cold War era. In the end, it may well pave the way for the capricious and inconsistent foreign-policy responses that have been labeled elsewhere as "bungee cord humanitarianism" (Bush 1996).

This chapter reviews the evolution of the crisis in Somalia and the international response in the form of the First United Nations Operation in Somalia (UNOSOM I), the UN Unified Task Force in Somalia (UNITAF), and the Second United Nations Operation in Somalia (UNOSOM II). The article develops the concept of a mission for peace as an aid to understanding and assessing large-scale, multifaceted, externally led humanitarian interventions. (This concept was introduced in a series of workshops sponsored by the Parliamentary Centre for Foreign Affairs and Foreign Trade in 1993 and 1994.) By developing this concept, we may not only improve our capacity to assess international responses to Somalia but also formulate better responses to other humanitarian crises when they arise — and, ideally, before they arise.

The most recent example of this type of operation was the short-lived Canadian-led initiative in late 1996 to establish a multinational force in eastern Zaire, as sanctioned by Security Council Resolution 1080 (in 1996). We should be clear about the context in which missions for peace are attempted. They are undertaken only after national and international actors have failed to resolve, defuse, or perhaps even just recognize those simmering tensions and conflicts that have usually followed a clear and unambiguous descent into violence. Mohamed Sahnoun, the former Special Representative of the Secretary-General (SRSG) to Somalia, has argued forcefully that the international community missed the opportunity to undertake preventive measures, both political and humanitarian, that would have saved the lives of hundreds of thousands of people and averted the tragedy that will scar generations of Somalis (Sahnoun 1994b).

This chapter examines some of the methodological and conceptual issues related to a mission for peace. It focuses on the evolution of the Somalia crisis and the subsequent international and Canadian responses. The chapter concludes with a discussion of lessons from the case that can be applied to similar challenges elsewhere in the world.

Missions for peace

The objective of a mission for peace is not a return to the status quo ante. A *status quo ante bellum* is rarely a desirable state of affairs. Also, in most cases, years of violent conflict and profound changes in the international political economy have destroyed any chance of returning to the status quo. The ultimate objective of a mission for peace is the creation of a new basis for peaceful coexistence. The end point of a mission is not the creation of a conflict-free utopia; rather, it is the creation of a society in which conflict may be dealt with nonviolently, as it arises, through sustainable, indigenous structures and processes.

Missions for peace are premised on the understanding that even in the most extreme cases of conflict, violence is rarely so undifferentiated or impenetrable that it completely forecloses all efforts to deconstruct the structures of violence and to reconstruct structures of peace. After years of studying conflict and discord in the Middle East, Azar (1986, pp. 30–31) came to the following conclusion:

> *Conflictual and cooperative events flow together even in the most severe of intense conflicts. Cooperative events are sometimes far more numerous than conflictual ones even in the midst of intense social conflict situations. However, conflictual events are clearly more absorbing and have more impact on determining the consequent actions of groups and nations [and one might add, on determining the outsider's impression of the conflict]. Cooperative events are not sufficient to abate protracted social conflicts. Tension reduction measures may make the conflict more bearable in the short term, but conflict resolution involves a far more complex process than mere conflict management.*

In other words, even in cases of severe, protracted conflict, local and international actors have the peaceful spaces in which to collectively engage in missions for peace. These spaces are fluid, tenuous, and dangerous but very much in existence. The optimization of the opportunities offered by these spaces requires sensitivity, creativity, and timing. These are precisely the spaces that are created by and catalyze the activities of a variety of community groups in conflict situations around the world. Such groups include citizens' committees, such as the Batticaloa Peace Committee in Sri Lanka; mothers' groups campaigning for the end of disappearances, such as the Mothers of Acari in Brazil; intercommunal peace-and-reconciliation groups, such as Corrymeela, the Cornerstone Community, PACE (Protestant and Catholic Encounter), and the Peace People in Northern Ireland; and many others.

Missions for peace may serve to consolidate and expand these "islands of peace," even in the midst of continuing violence. The importance of this process is threefold. First, it empowers peace-seeking groups and individuals to begin to establish alternative and accommodating bases for structuring social relations that challenge the brutal might-is-right ethos of the predominant system. Second, it encourages the development of a partnership between international and local actors and may thereby increase the efficacy of a mission for peace and its chances for success. Finally, and related to the last point, both the cultivation and the expansion of peace-seeking segments of society add to the sustainability of the results of the mission.

The concept of a mission for peace needs to be added to the debates about Boutros-Ghali's (1992) *Agenda for Peace*. A conspicuous limitation of Boutros-Ghali's position paper is its insistence on maintaining the state as the principal actor in international peace efforts. Although state actors undoubtedly are central to some of these efforts, they are neither the only nor necessarily the most important actors. Nonstate actors are also playing central roles in international responses to conflicts attracting international attention — from the crucial role of civilians in the UN mission in Cambodia to the front-line humanitarian role of nongovernmental organizations (NGOs) in Rwanda, Zaire, and other areas of conflict around the world.

This chapter adopts Korten's (1990) structural and operational definition of an NGO; that is, an NGO is an organization with the following characteristics:

- *Formal existence* — The organization is institutionalized to some extent (it is formalized in terms of regular meetings, office bearers, and some degree of organizational permanence);
- *Private status* — The organization is institutionally separate from government, although it may receive some government support;

- *Nonprofit-distributing modis operandi* — Although the organization may generate a financial surplus, this does not accrue to the owners or directors;
- *Self-governing* — The organization is able and equipped to control and manage its own activities; and
- *Voluntary character* — There is some meaningful degree of voluntary participation in the conduct or management of the organization. (This does not mean that all or most of the income of an organization must come from voluntary contributions or that most of its staff must be volunteers.)

Missions for peace require that both state and nonstate actors, such as NGOs, participate not only in the implementation phase of a mission but also in the planning, formulation, and decision-making phases.

Although Boutros-Ghali reinvigorated and delineated peacekeeping, peacemaking, peacebuilding, and preventive diplomacy, the cases acting as the major points of reference in contemporary international politics involve a combination of these activities. Thus, the concept of a mission for peace in this chapter is rooted in the belief that any successful peace initiative must necessarily include elements from all of these areas of action. It is important to distinguish each of these four types of activity conceptually and operationally, but a central idea in a mission for peace is that the success of a peace initiative is more than the sum of the separate impacts of each of these activities. Success depends on the ways the different components of these types of intervention mesh with each other and (as importantly) with existing social, political, and economic structures in war-torn societies. To the extent these pieces fit together, the likelihood of an effective intervention is increased. Conversely, to the extent they fail to fit together, there is a danger that such interventions may be ineffective, or worse, counterproductive. As others have pointed out, the minimum requirement of international actors in conflict-prone settings is that they "do no harm" through their interventions (Anderson 1996).

As noted above, missions for peace are made up of a variety of both actors and activities. However, it should be clear that some types of actors are better suited to playing particular roles in each of the areas specified by Boutros-Ghali. Peacekeeping is best undertaken by military actors. Clearly, peacekeeping operations have increasingly employed civilians in their activities. However, this does not challenge the understanding that peacekeeping is best undertaken by military personnel;

rather, it raises the question of whether the "changing nature of peacekeeping operations" is pushing peacekeepers from peacekeeping and into activities for which they may not be suited or into activities better undertaken by other actors (Bush 1995). The formal political actors and organizations, including political leaders, statesmen, and stateswomen, as well as recognized and accepted leaders of the groups involved in a conflict, are best suited to tackle peacemaking and preventive diplomacy. Peacebuilding falls most clearly within the purview of private-sector actors, NGOs, community organizations, and so on. Therefore, just as NGOs should not be expected to play a peacekeeping role, the military, as conventionally constituted, should not be expected to play a peacebuilding role. In missions for peace, the success of one activity is often related to the success of the others. Although these types of activities may be interdependent, they are not interchangeable. By focusing broadly on missions for peace, one is better able to understand the linkages between these distinct but interrelated activities.

Because missions for peace encompass such diverse types of activity, the scope of their activities in the security, political, and socioeconomic arenas is broad. Such activities may include the stabilization of security; provision of humanitarian relief; brokering of local, national, and international peace agreements; cultivation of appropriate and acceptable political and economic institutions; rehabilitation; reconstruction; and reconciliation. Each of these activities is but one component of a mission for peace. By considering these as a whole, one comes closer to understanding the phenomenon of a mission for peace.

Was the operation in Somalia a mission for peace? Yes, the operation was a mission for peace: it possessed many of the components discussed above. However, it was a failed mission for peace. As such, it may teach us as much about what not to do as about what we should do when confronted by similar challenges in the future.

The Evolution of Crisis in Somalia

The media have tended to characterize Somalia as a brutal "war of all against all" — a Hobbesian world where human action is motivated entirely by selfish concerns and where the desire for security is inseparable from the desire for power pursued through the use of force (Makinda 1993, p. 29). Although this characterization serves to highlight one facet of the dynamic of violence that has escalated steadily in Somalia, it simultaneously obscures traditional forms of conflict management (such as elder-based systems) that have addressed disputes nonviolently both before and during the concerted international intervention. Furthermore, the Hobbesian world-view makes the individual the basic political unit, but the Somalian world-view is deeply grounded in the clan. In Somalia, it is the social network, rather than the individual, that constitutes the bedrock of social, political, and economic life. This is the social reality that must orient international responses in Somalia and in other regions with similar kinds of social structures. Although the Hobbesian conception of anarchy is an inaccurate characterization of Somalia, a broader political-realist conception of the term may be appropriate if it is understood to refer generally to a system lacking a central authority capable of imposing order or control. *Anarchy* in this sense has been used by political realists of all stripes to describe an essential feature of the international system. Using *anarchy* in this sense, one can describe international intervention in Somalia as the meeting of two anarchies — one international, the other intranational.

The Somali Republic came into being in 1960 as a result of the merger of the British Somaliland protectorate and the Italian Trusteeship Territory of Somalia. The analysis in this chapter begins with the successful coup by Major General Mohamed Siyad Barre in 1969. Notwithstanding the importance of the pre-Barre period, the discussion begins with the Barre regime because it (aided and abetted by international actors) established the foundation for the intensity and destructiveness of the conflict that followed. Like previous Somali leaders after independence, Barre established a support network based on nepotism, clan allegiances, and connections (for example, Barre's son-in-law was variously the head of the National Security Services, Interior Minister, and Assistant Secretary General of the ruling party). By playing off clans and subclans, Barre fueled factional power struggles as a means of defusing opposition to his rule. He concentrated power in his own hands, cracked down on dissent, weakened the civil service, and politicized the military.

Economic conditions in the country deteriorated, as a result of both Barre's rule and the ravages of the international political economy. According to World Bank figures for Somalia, the gross national product (GNP) per capita was US $80 in 1970, $150 in 1976, and only $120 in 1990. The same pattern of economic stagnation is evident in those African countries defined by the World Bank as low-income nations. Among this group, the average GNP per capita dropped from US $490 to $260 (a loss of 40%) between 1980 and 1990 (Weil 1993). Makinda (1993, p. 45) accurately described Somalia's economic predicament: "there has been so much disruption that it is possible to describe Somalia's economy only in terms of the past and its potential. Its present is represented by disorders and uncertainties."

During the Barre regime, interclan conflicts were militarized. The large quantity of arms amplifying the impact of violence and inhibiting conflict-management efforts in Somalia is the legacy of superpower rivalry during the Cold War. The importance of the Horn of Africa in the strategic calculations of the Soviet Union and United States in the 1970s and 1980s enabled Barre to play the two against each other so as to amass a substantial arsenal. According to Makinda (1993), by the mid-1970s — when the Soviet–Somali friendship was at its apex — Somalia possessed the best-equipped armed forces in sub-Saharan Africa. In 1977, Barre conveniently shuffled allegiances, expelled the Soviets, and made way for US military support. By 1990, under tutelage of the United States, Somalia had built up a military force of more than 65 000 personnel. In proportion to its population at the time (6 million), the Somali military force was huge by African standards.

The "militarization" of Somali society not only refers to the size of the military and the influx of weapons into streets and fields, but also refers to the tendency for intergroup relations and conflict to be defined in narrow military terms. Typically, this tendency coincides with an increase in military-related expenditures and a crackdown on even minor expressions of dissent. More generally, militarization is a phenomenon in which political problems come to be represented as military problems and, by extension, are seen to require military solutions. (The militarization of rule remained conspicuous even when Barre attempted to apply a civilian political veneer to his regime. For example, in 1981, 68 of the 85 new district and regional party secretaries were from either the military or the police [Makinda 1993].)

Increasingly, Barre was attacked by opponents (including some within the military), particularly following his military adventurism that led to the defeat of the Somali armed forces by Ethiopia in the war of 1977/78. In April 1978, a failed coup was launched against Barre by a subclan that had been excluded from central power. Attacks against the Barre regime occurred as shifts in interclan coalitions began to erode Barre's ability to maintain a support base. Two dangerous and related processes were evident during this period: the "ethnicization" of the Somali military forces and the militarization of clan-based groupings. As Makinda (1993, p. 24) explains it,

> *Problems in the military became obvious in the late 1980s as feuding between rival generals and their clans hampered the army's ability to*

fight the rebels. The army's problems were exacerbated by the fact that in the 1980s, recruitment proceeded along clan lines, with new recruits being put into units from their own areas and under officers from their own clans. As a result, by the late 1980s, there was no clear difference between regular army units and clan militias.

By 1988, violent opposition to the Barre regime had coalesced into a savage civil war, with all the attendant atrocities: the targeting and massacre of civilians, the indiscriminate use of land mines, the poisoning of wells, and the slaughter of livestock. Between May 1988 and December 1989, 50 000–60 000 people were killed in the violence — most were members of the Issaq clan, an anti-Barre group from northern Somalia (AWC 1990). Violence escalated as brutality and human-rights abuses perpetrated by one armed gang were matched (and often surpassed) by those of another. It was estimated that 450 000 Somalis fled to Ethiopia, seeking refuge, and 600 000 were internally displaced (CIIPS 1990).

Because power had been centralized in Barre's hands for almost 20 years, the few existing political institutions functioned principally as an extension of his personal rule. Thus, one would have no reason to expect even minimal institutional continuity when Barre left the political stage. Not surprisingly then, when Barre was overthrown in January 1991, no real state institutions existed to be taken over. However, even if such institutions had existed, no group (or coalition of groups) was powerful enough to seize control or popular enough to win it. Following a fleeting period of post-Barre optimism in Somalia, violent interclan and intraclan rivalries were reignited in rural and urban areas. Although many people in the diplomatic community left the country following the fall of Barre, several NGOs and international organizations stayed on to respond to the needs of Somalis, despite changing and uncertain political and security environments. These organizations included the Cooperative for American Relief Everywhere (CARE), the Oxford Committee for Famine Relief (OXFAM), Médecins sans frontières (Doctors without Borders), the Mennonite Central Committee, the International Committee of the Red Cross (ICRC), the International Federation of the Red Cross and Red Crescent Societies, the United Nations Children's Fund (UNICEF), the UN High Commission for Refugees (UNHCR), the UN Department of Humanitarian Affairs, and the World Food Programme (WFP).

Without an overarching system of political control within Somalia, self-protection became necessary, and self-aggrandizement by marauding bands of clan-based militias became rampant. Power and authority resided predominantly in clan-based warlords and their gunmen. The leaders of the main armed factions in Somalia were the following:[1]

- The late Muhammad Farrah Aideed, the major warlord of the Hawiye clan, who controlled most of the territory in southern Somalia, as well as that in southern Mogadishu (in late 1990, his forces invaded Somalia from their base in Ethiopia, helping to push Barre from power);
- Ali Mahdi Muhammed, also a member of the Hiwaye clan, who declared himself interim president of Somalia and controlled northern Mogadishu and a narrow strip of land running north from the city;
- Muhammad Said Hersi Morgan, the son-in-law of Barre and a member of the Darod clan, which controlled the city of Bardera (or Baardheere), located in the centre of the famine region;
- Colonel Omar Jess, also a member of the Darod clan, who controlled the strategic port of Kismayu in southern Somalia; and
- General Muhammad Abshir Musa, leader of the Somali Democratic Front, one of the first organizations to oppose Barre (Musa controlled an area in northeastern Somalia).

The "power of the gun" became the basis for the authority of warlords, displacing the traditional system based on clan elders. A fluid and volatile environment arose, in which armed groups sought to protect or expand their territorial and resource base. Wollacott (cited in Gordon 1994, pp. 286–287) described the differences between old rivalries and new forms of conflict as follows:

> *[It was] a new kind of social violence, still clan-based, but with vicious differences. First, the main actors were not traditional "big men" from the clans, but upstart leaders without the same responsibilities or backgrounds. Second, the fighting was mechanized, machine guns replaced rifles. Third, traditional institutions which had mitigated and mediated clan rivalries, like the blood price system, had withered away. Fourth, the violence was now commercially sustained by a complex trade in which drugs, mainly the local favourite qat, and food, including aid shipments, are traded off for the fuel, ammunition, and other supplies necessary to maintain armies and patronage structures of the warlords.*

---

[1] For further details on the factional leaders, see The Economist (1993); for a discussion of the intricacies of clan groups and interclan politics, see Makinda (1993).

The clan rivalries exacerbated by Barre's regime are evident in the pattern of violence in Somalia today. On one level, Somali politics appear to have reverted to those of precolonial times, when clans and subclans fought and formed alliances in a series of perpetual skirmishes to maintain control of roughly defined parcels of land. However, one finds two fundamental differences in the more recent situation. First, the pervasiveness of powerful weapons profoundly increases the destructive and disruptive force of inter- and intraclan rivalry. Second, an equally profound change has occurred in the international context in which such corrosive types of conflict take place. The first difference has amplified the sense of anarchy in Somalia, and the second difference (as discussed below) made possible an unprecedented international intervention in a humanitarian crisis.

Somalia has always depended on erratic rainfall for its food supply. The country was again in the midst of a severe drought in late 1991. This, combined with the civil war, caused agricultural production to plummet. Food production in Somalia was estimated to be at only 30% of its normal level (Kunder 1992). The situation became increasingly desperate as hunger and starvation became conspicuous weapons of war. Armed factions prevented aid agencies from delivering food and humanitarian assistance. The looting of food convoys and feeding stations seriously hindered humanitarian efforts. In March 1992, the ICRC (cited in Leaning 1993, p. 114) reported "horrifying" levels (90%) of moderate to severe malnutrition in the populations around Beledweyne and Marka. It was estimated that of the 4.5-million Somali population south of the disputed territory of Somaliland, one-third, or 1.5 million people, were at serious risk of death from starvation over a 6-month period.

By the fall of 1991, the areas in and around Mogadishu had become a war zone. Armed groups launched massive artillery attacks on areas controlled by rivals in different parts of the city. Throughout the country, war had devastated much of Somalia's physical infrastructure, especially bridges, schools, airports, and hospitals. For the period of mid-November 1991 to February 1992, an estimated 1 200 people per week were killed outright or died of their injuries, and another 2 500 were surviving wounded; the number of casualties reached 41 000 for this 11-week period (see Leaning 1993).

By February 1992, the military confrontation had reached a stalemate, despite heavy nighttime artillery barrages and sporadic daytime barrages. Mogadishu was cleaved in two, each section controlled by one of the major warlords and their respective clans. The southern two-thirds of the city, including the hills overlooking the harbour, was controlled by Ali Madhi (see Leaning 1993).

As early as 1990, NGOs were warning of looming catastrophe in Somalia, and clearly the violence had been festering for considerably longer than that. But the international community was distracted by events elsewhere, especially in the Middle East and in the former Yugoslavia. Analysts reached a general consensus that the international community was very slow to respond to the conflict in Somalia. Despite the long-time activities of multilateral agencies and NGOs in Somalia, broader UN involvement did not begin until January 1992, when Boutros Boutros-Ghali, the former Egyptian minister of state for foreign affairs, who had a long-standing interest in the Horn of Africa, became the UN Secretary-General. By mid-1992, the UN began to take a more prominent role in organizing the delivery of humanitarian assistance.

A bolt from the blue: Canada–Somalia relations before and after UNOSOM

Before examining the Canadian role in the large-scale UN missions in Somalia, it is important to consider Canada's relationship with Somalia before the international humanitarian interventions. This will help to shed light on the broader context and implications for Canadian foreign policy.

Canada–Somalia relations were decidedly ambivalent, despite the presence of Canadian NGOs in the Horn of Africa for decades before Canadian participation in the UNOSOM–UNITAF missions. In many ways, Somalia was invisible on the Canadian foreign-policy landscape before UN intervention. The annual reports of External Affairs in 1980–90 contain only two sentences making direct reference to Somalia. The annual reports of the Canadian Institute for International Peace and Security illustrate the same point. References to the Horn of Africa (a parcel of countries in East Africa) in House of Commons debates and other governmental forums focus more directly on Ethiopia than on Somalia. Somalia's lack of political presence in Canadian foreign policy may have been partly related to Somalia's lack of economic presence as an international trading partner.[2] It may have also been due to the Cold

[2] The ranking of Somalia among African countries receiving Canadian exports was as follows: in 1985, 33rd of 35 ($148 000); in 1986, 29th of 35 ($1.817 million); in 1987, 30th of 35 ($825 000); and in 1988, 30th of 35 ($490 000) (EAITC 1988/89).

War; that is, given the superpower overlay of politics in the Horn of Africa, the Canadian government may have self-consciously maintained a low profile in the region.

Recent data from the Canadian International Development Agency (CIDA) offer a more nuanced description of the Canada–Somalia relationship. From 1974 to the end of the 1990/91 fiscal year, Canada contributed $135.95 million in official development assistance (ODA) for humanitarian and development work in Somalia. This assistance was distributed through the following channels: $15.9 million in bilateral food aid; $50 million in multilateral food aid; $31 million through international financial institutions; $10 million in humanitarian assistance; and $15 million through other multilateral channels (CIDA 1994). However, from January 1990 to December 1993 — that is, throughout the crisis discussed above — Canada provided $42.8 million in food aid and nonfood assistance to Somalia and Somali refugees in the Horn of Africa. In other words, a very significant portion of Canadian ODA to Somalia was delivered in the last 3 of the past 20 years, when Canada was an active participant in the UN mission. Despite the impressive cumulative total amount, Canadian ODA to Somalia before this period was on average $5.18 million a year. These data support the view that Somalia was not an especially important consideration in the foreign-policy calculations of the Canadian government before 1991. If this is so, why did the Canadian government choose to participate so vigorously, so suddenly?

The main factors motivating the Canadian government to respond to the conflict in Somalia were the same as those underpinning its involvement in the Ethiopian famine-relief efforts of the 1980s. Most significant was the public pressure fanned by the media coverage of the human face of the catastrophe. Mohamed Sahnoun was especially appreciative of the media for its role in attracting international attention and rallying international resources (see Sahnoun 1994b). The rallying of international attention through the media generated bottom-up pressure on the Canadian government. When a growing domestic constituency began to demand Canadian involvement, the government recognized the need to be seen to be responding to the now-public crisis. Thus, a crucial motivation for the large-scale Canadian response, through the UN, was the need for the government of the day to maintain public (that is, electoral) support. Interestingly, Boulton (1994) argued that this was a motivating factor for US-government involvement as well. In addition to the pressure from below — to be seen to be responding — the Canadian government was pressured from above by actors in the international community. UN requests for Canadian participation in its missions provided the government with the opportunity to defuse pressure from both above and below while maintaining its traditional support for multilateralism, the UN system in particular. As discussed below, it appeared that the Canadian decision to participate in the UN mission was expedited by the perception among some advisers and decision-makers that it seemed doable.

I do not wish to downplay the humanitarian aspect of the Canadian government's response. However, the fact remains that other humanitarian crises of equal or greater devastation did not attract equivalent attention. Humanitarianism alone does not prompt government action. Implicit and explicit cost–benefit calculations factor in perceived or actual changes in levels of domestic political support; opportunities to achieve political gains or avoid political losses and to tap new sources of political capital; and other such considerations.

Once the political will was in place, Canada massively increased its volume of assistance to Somalia, especially through multilateral channels. Significantly, the volume of assistance appeared to drop as precipitously as it rose (personal interviews with CIDA personnel, Hull, PQ, Canada, spring 1994). There are a number of possible explanations for this. A cynical, yet realistic, suggestion would be that Somalia may have lost its salience in Canadian domestic politics after it faded from the headlines. Just as the arrival of the Americans had pushed the conflict in Somalia onto the main stage, their exit pulled it into the wings. The departure of the Americans was followed by that of almost every peacekeeping contingent from developed countries. Another explanation is based on the law of supply and demand: by 1994, the food pipeline into Somalia had become congested. A basic emergency food-distribution system was in place, although it continued to be stressed by demand and looting by bandits. However temporarily, mass starvation had been postponed. Despite the easing of the immediate food crisis, the underlying causes remained unaffected, and, as significantly, violence seemed to be increasing. As a result, many NGOs and multilateral agencies pulled out or scaled down their operations. Thus, the reduction of direct Canadian assistance was also likely related to the fact that many aid agencies pulled out of Somalia because of the hazardous security situation. In April 1994, the general security situation was described by the WFP as "unstable and unpredictable with sporadic shooting, sniping, and kidnapping incidents" (WFP 1994). During that period, UNICEF and UNHCR food convoys were ambushed and looted; an Indian peacekeeper was shot dead; and some WFP field operations had been forced to close because of armed attacks on its convoys and offices. Similarly, interclan violence forced a number of international organizations (including UNICEF, Claritas, and Intersos) to evacuate personnel from fighting zones. The response of Nobel laureate Elie Wiesel to a question on the Bosnian civil war applies equally to Somalia: to the question, "What light [does] the holocaust throw on the Bosnian civil war?" he responded, "No light — only shadows. All I can say is that the human condition is so fragile that the impossible is indeed possible. The unthinkable can indeed come to pass, for good as well as evil. We always have a choice" (*The Gazette* [Montréal], 18 June 1994, p. A1).

Thus, despite a significant Canadian-government contribution to the multinational missions to Somalia, the conflict limped on.

When two anarchies meet

The dynamics of conflict among clans and subclans in Somalia was mirrored in less violent ways in the relations between the international actors involved in relief operations, especially those under the auspices of the UN. The squabbling and turf fights among and between UN and non-UN actors in Somalia became increasingly public as the operation expanded in size and scope. (Similar criticisms were made concerning UN operations in the former Jugoslavia by retired Major General Lewis MacKenzie, former commander of UN forces in Sarajevo [Whig Standard 1993]). Some of the most penetrating criticisms of the UN operation in Somalia came from Mohamed Sahnoun, the former SRSG to Somalia. He was reported to have said that the failure of relief operations was due to "an overwhelming United Nations bureaucracy that, in contrast to the Red Cross, is made up of civil servants more interested in careers and perquisites than in the job at hand" (*The New York Times*, 7 September 1992, p. A3). As discussed below, this has clear implications for the efficacy of a mission for peace or for any smaller scale UN intervention in a humanitarian crisis.

The UN responses to Somalia in 1992 had a discernible pattern. The year was marked by a series of Security Council resolutions that were passed but subsequently deemed ineffective and replaced by new ones. Through this process, the Security Council became increasingly prominent and interventionist in Somalia. Its resolutions spanned the range of options, from a complete weapons embargo in January 1992 to armed humanitarian intervention by the end of the year.

UNOSOM I was authorized by Security Council Resolution 751 on 24 April 1992. This operation followed from the failed February 1992 cease-fire agreement brokered by the UN, the Organization of African Unity, the Arab League, and the Islamic Conference. Although the agreement was signed by the leaders of the main warring factions (Aideed and Ali Madhi), it was summarily ignored by the warriors in each camp. Fighting continued unabated as factions blocked the delivery of humanitarian assistance to Somalis in increasingly desperate conditions throughout the country. In response to the lack of cooperation by combatants, the Secretary-General dispatched a UN technical team to Somalia to study the possibility of sending military observers. Canadian representatives supported the efforts by the Security Council to rally and direct an international response to the events in Somalia. This was reflected in the appointment of Robert Gallagher, a Canadian, to head the technical team sent to Somalia to assess the situation.

Resolution 751 called for the establishment of a peacekeeping force to provide security for humanitarian activities in Mogadishu. This was to include 50 unarmed military observers to monitor the cease-fire agreement in the city. After much haggling between UN representatives and clan factions, UN troops were eventually deployed. On paper, the number of peacekeepers was increased by a few hundred, but on the ground the UNOSOM I force never grew substantially. Importantly, Resolution 751 also agreed in principle to the idea of a UN force to escort the delivery of humanitarian aid.

Canada was one of 39 countries at the October 1992 UN donor conference in Geneva. The conference produced a 100-day accelerated plan for Somalia that was intended to expedite and better coordinate international humanitarian efforts. By late October, it was clear that the new plan was not working as intended. Armed factions continued to obstruct and loot humanitarian aid, in addition to extorting aid from international humanitarian organizations in southern and central Somalia. It quickly became apparent that the small UN peacekeeping contingent was unable to ensure that humanitarian aid was delivered throughout the country.

Following the ineffective UNOSOM I mission, Secretary-General Boutros-Ghali sought to launch a UN operation with a functioning military enforcement mechanism by invoking chapter VII of the *Charter of the United Nations* (for a thorough discussion of the reinterpretations of the Charter and the legal dimensions and implications of UN operations in Somalia, see Hutchinson [1993]). James Jonah, UN Undersecretary-General for Political Affairs at the time, was candid in his discussion of the Security Council debate on the Secretary-General's request for what amounted to armed humanitarian intervention (Jonah 1992). One particularly striking feature of the debate was the degree to which the previously inviolable principle of state sovereignty was not a constraint on the Council's decision-making. In fact, a precedent had already been set in the spring of 1991 when troops drawn from France, Italy, the Netherlands, Spain, the United Kingdom, and the United States participated in a NATO intervention in northern Iraq to protect 4 000–5 000 Kurds from attack by Saddam Hussein's military forces (Mackinlay 1993). In the end, UNITAF was chosen as the most appropriate response for Somalia. This US-led force of 30 000 troops from 23 countries was authorized by Security Council Resolution 794, on 3 December 1992, "to use all necessary means to establish as soon as possible a secure environment for humanitarian relief operations in Somalia" (UN 1992b), in particular, the protection of relief convoys from looting by clan-based militias. Although UNITAF was UN endorsed, it was not UN controlled. It was not until UNOSOM II that troops fell under the direct control of the Secretary-General — although the operation remained US dominated until the Americans pulled out in March 1994.

Resolution 794 has profound implications for international humanitarian law. Traditionally, the UN claimed the right to use force only in response to an illegal act of aggression by one state against another, such as in the case of Iraq in 1990/91. In the case of Somalia, however, the Security Council circumvented the implied requirement that the UN obtain the consent of a government before entering its territory, citing the destabilizing potential of widespread famine and continued civil war in Somalia as a threat to international peace. The resolution (UN 1992b, p. 1) expressed

> *great alarm at continuing reports of widespread violations of international humanitarian law occurring in Somalia, including reports of violence and threats of violence against personnel participating lawfully in impartial humanitarian relief activities; deliberate attacks on non-combatants, relief consignments and vehicles, and medical and relief facilities; and, impeding the delivery of food and medical supplies essential for the survival of the civilian population.*

Some members of the Security Council hesitated to intervene in the domestic politics of a state (even a failed state) without a formal request from political representatives, but their reservations were conveniently overcome through the creation and use of what Jonah (1993, p. 72) called a "legal fiction": a Somali request for UN intervention arrived "in the form of a letter from the Somali charge d'affaires in New York who, in reality, represented no one" (see also UN 1992a).

The idea of a large-scale armed humanitarian operation stood in contrast to the approach pursued by the SRSG to Somalia, Mohamed Sahnoun, a seasoned Algerian diplomat appointed by the Secretary-General in April 1992. The Secretary-General's top-down interventionist strategy was compatible with Washington's desired option (Jonah 1993). Indeed, this strategy would not have been feasible without Washington's full support. However, it did not fit with Sahnoun's own approach, which was to seek political settlement and national reconciliation in Somalia through existing social and political structures, such as elder-based authority systems, rather than rule by gun. In northern Somalia, Sahnoun negotiated an agreement with the administration of the self-declared "Republic of Somaliland," an agreement that would have introduced 350 UN soldiers into the region to ensure that supply routes to northeast and central Somalia remained open for food aid. In return, the UN would be committed to repairing local infrastructure in the region (Makinda 1993). Sahnoun favoured a gradual approach that worked within the existing social and political structures to modify those very same structures. Yet, Boutros-Ghali's insistence that Somaliland be treated as part of Somalia undercut an incremental, regionally based approach to conflict settlement.

This difference in approach led to the resignation of Sahnoun and the appointment of a new SRSG, Ismat Kittani, who was able to assess the Somalia situation in a way that was compatible with the Secretary-General's desired option. Thus, in November 1992, Kittani wrote a letter to the Secretary-General requesting international intervention. Boutros-Ghali took this letter to President Bush. The Sahnoun–Boutros-Ghali disagreement was indicative of tensions within the UN and, more importantly, of competing approaches to the settlement of violent conflict, the delivery of humanitarian assistance, and long-term development strategies. Not surprisingly, Sahnoun's assessment of the situation echoed that of many NGOs and Somalis: "the perception that the role of the UN presence has shifted from a humanitarian one to that of an 'occupying force' is widespread among Somalis" (Watson 1993).

Canada demonstrated its support for Resolution 794 by making a military contribution to the operation. By the first week of January 1993, a Canadian contingent of more than 1 300 personnel was in the field. Operation Deliverance principally comprised the Canadian Airborne Regiment of Petawawa. The force was based in Beledweyne

(Belet Huen) and was responsible for protecting humanitarian operations within a sector of 30 000 square kilometres. The supply vessel HMCS *Preserver* was stationed off Mogadishu to provide logistical, medical, and helicopter support for Canadian operations. Equipment, vehicles, and supplies were delivered by 18 air crews and a number of aircraft from CFB Trenton (DFA 1993). A flight of six CH-135 helicopters was also stationed in Somalia to provide reconnaissance and logistical support.

In addition to Canada's participation in the UNITAF, Canadian Forces launched Operation Relief, a humanitarian airlift undertaken from September 1992 to late February 1993.[3] The operation was part of Canada's response to the UN appeal for emergency assistance to Somalia. Three Canadian Forces C-130 Hercules transport planes and some 70 Canadian military personnel from the 429 and 436 squadrons (CFB Trenton) and the 435 Squadron (CFB Edmonton) were based in Nairobi, Kenya, to support the humanitarian efforts, in particular those of the WFP and the ICRC. In total, 550 flights were required to deliver 7.44 million kg of food from Kenya to more than 20 locations in Somalia (DFA 1993). During this operation, Canadian Forces earned a reputation for their commitment and ability to "do the impossible" in the delivery of food aid. In the course of my discussions with an official in the High Commission in Nairobi, the two-way radio in his office provided a continuous background of exchanges between NGOs or UN agencies and High Commission staff as they coordinated airlifts. It was explained to me that many aid workers found that bureaucratic requirements inhibited the use of US transport planes to deliver aid. Consequently, many aid workers turned to the Canadians, who seemed to never turn anything away and always delivered the goods to location.

CARE Canada was an especially active player in international relief operations in Somalia. In addition to its ongoing activities in Somalia, it was subcontracted by the WFP to deliver food aid in Somalia. The scale of the increase in CARE Canada's involvement in Somalia was reflected in the increase in its support and revenue income to $130.8 million in the fiscal year ending 30 June 1993 from $57.8 million in the previous fiscal year. During this period, support for its projects increased to $90 million from $31 million. The increase

---

[3] The Canadian Armed Forces had acquired expertise in humanitarian airlifts in the Horn of Africa when it played a vital role in the UN airlift operation to Ethiopia, which began in August 1991. Two Canadian Hercules aircraft from the Air Transport Group of the Canadian Forces and about 60 personnel operated out of Djibouti to deliver 15 million kg of food and supplies to different regions in Ethiopia — almost half the total amount airlifted in the UN operation (DND 1991a, b).

included almost $72 million in grain (made available by the WFP and other donors), most of which was distributed in Somalia (CARE Canada 1993).

The support for the intervention option displaced the arguments of those favouring a UN-sponsored, bottom-up approach. The debate, which did not occur at that time, should be placed centrally in the discussions currently taking place concerning humanitarian interventions. Are the international community and Canada willing to make a long-term commitment to support the gradual evolution of peace in countries like Somalia? Or are they tied to the short-term, low-risk, high-profile interventions? Do alternatives exist somewhere in the middle, such as augmented support for NGOs?

The UNITAF troops were largely successful in meeting their primary military task: to open supply routes for the delivery of humanitarian aid. Yet, there was considerable disgruntlement over the US refusal to disarm Somali militias, despite the Secretary-General's insistence that this task was central to the UNITAF mandate and a prerequisite to handing the operation back to the UN. The US definition of security was more narrow than the Secretary-General's and applied to only 40% of Somali territory (Makinda 1993; Bolton 1994). In late 1994, one could observe a striking parallel between the refusal of the US military to disarm warriors in Somalia and its reluctance in Haiti to disarm police and soldiers loyal to the junta of Lieutenant-General Raoul Cedras. Thus, as US troops disembarked from their warships, they were met with the spectacle of pro-US Haitians being savagely beaten by Haitian police. The US military had not articulated its rules of engagement for dealing with "Haitian-on-Haitian violence" (*Globe and Mail,* 21 September 1994, pp. A1, A10).

The Canadian Forces in Beledweyne fulfilled its military mission of making the region safe for humanitarian operations. It is also important to point out that the Canadian soldiers were engaged in activities that went far beyond their UNITAF mandate. Canadian Forces doctors and dentists donated their time to hospitals in Mogadishu and Beledweyne. Canadian peacekeepers helped to reestablish four schools in Beledweyne and one school in each of four other communities. This involved not only building some of the schools from the ground up but also finding Somali teachers to staff them. The staffing problem was solved when the peacekeepers teamed up with a US NGO able to help find Somali teachers and acquire the necessary teaching supplies. In Mogadishu, Canadian Forces technicians repaired equipment for NGOs and for the Medina hospital. The support staff on the HMCS

Preserver would go ashore to Mogadishu daily to collect broken machinery from hospitals, schools, and shops. This broken machinery would be brought aboard the ship, repaired, and returned within a few days. Similar operations were undertaken by engineering staff in Beledweyne. Canadian Forces also repaired roads and runways in their assignment areas. Canadian peacekeepers were especially successful in initiating a training program for a local police force in Beledweyne — a task crucial to ensuring the community's sense of confidence in those responsible for law and order. The argument has been made that the "Canadian effort may be a model for rebuilding [Somalia]" (York 1993).

Unfortunately, much of the media coverage of Canadian peacekeepers in Somalia has concentrated on the brutal torture and murder of a Somali while under Canadian Forces custody. This event tarnishes the reputation of every Canadian peacekeeper, past and present. It should not, however, completely obscure the wider contributions of Canadian peacekeepers. By most accounts, the Canadians developed an excellent rapport with the local Somali community because they were willing to roll up their sleeves and get down to work with the local Somalis. (The same observation has been made of the Canadian peacekeepers in Bosnia [*Globe and Mail*, 21 September 1994, pp. A1, A2].) One officer recounted a story of members of the Airborne Regiment waste deep in the mud of the banks of the Wabi Shebele river helping a farmer extricate his camel. A portable crane and a sling finally succeeded in freeing the frantic animal. The point is not that the Canadian military role in Somalia was without problems but that it is inaccurate to characterize the entire Canadian peacekeeping mission with exclusive reference to an inexcusable incident of ill-discipline. To do so would obscure the constructive lessons that may be at least tentatively drawn.

The argument here is not that Canadian peacekeepers achieved their military objectives because of their extramandate activities but that such activities reduced the potential friction of introducing a foreign military force. These activities played crucial supporting roles in the military mandate of Canadian peacekeepers. Although such actions were a tribute to the commitment of the Canadian peacekeepers, it would be inaccurate to define them as peacebuilding efforts. Their short-term, interventionary character and the specific capacities of the executing actors locate these activities within the peacekeeping realm. They would become peacebuilding activities if they sought to cultivate the indigenous capacities needed to achieve the same results in a way that built sustainable, constructive bridges between communities. This point needs to be emphasized because it bears on the recent efforts of the Canadian military to justify budgetary continuity by repackaging itself as a jack of all trades. Such efforts both neglect and inflate the institutional and corporate capacities of national military organization. The Canadian Department of National Defence, like the military organizations of most other states, was organized for a world seen through the prism of the Cold War. In the context of the fundamental changes in the international political and economic system since the fall of the Soviet Union, it is a truism that armed forces need to be restructured to correspond to new security realities. The defence-policy review is an attempt to do just this. Suggestions regarding future Canadian peacekeeping efforts are presented below.

Significant changes occurred in the transition from UNITAF to UNOSOM II. UNOSOM II was the largest and most expensive UN-controlled peacekeeping operation in history. It comprised more than 33 000 troops (including 1 250 Canadians) from more than 20 countries. Its first-year operations were expected to cost US $1.5 billion. Most importantly, significant changes occurred in the mandate. Whereas UNITAF was directed by the US military under the auspices of the UN, UNOSOM II was the first enforcement operation to be directly under the control of the Secretary-General. It was the first UN peacekeeping operation to have a mandate to employ force in the pursuit of UN objectives. It stood in stark contrast to the traditional peacekeeping model, in which force was sanctioned only in self-defence. Resolution 837 of 6 June 1993 reaffirmed UNOSOM II's mandate to take all necessary measures to implement agreements reached and to arrest, detain, try, and punish those who attempted to frustrate the UN mission (UN 1993). This expanded mandate led inevitably to direct and assertive confrontations with Somali factions, the results of which were reported in the media — usually more widely when there were casualties among UN troops (for a discussion of North–South divisions between UN peacekeepers, see Dyer [1993]). Between 5 June and 5 September 1993, 46 UN troops were killed, along with more than 300 Somali children, women, and men.

The US dominance of the UNITAF and UNOSOM II mission drew criticism from countries like Italy, which felt that it deserved a more prominent role in the UN operations because of its past colonial connections with the Horn of Africa. US dominance was partly related to the fact that the United States had initially provided the largest contingent of troops for the peacekeeping component of the operation, including a significant logistical element. Americans were central to the top levels of the operation. Although the first UNOSOM II commander was from Turkey, he was nominated by the United States; his deputy was an American Major General who, coincidentally, was also tactical commander of the 1 700-member American Rapid Deployment Unit — the unit that carried out the well-publicized and unsuccessful raids to capture Somali warlord Mohamed Aideed. The SRSG in 1993 was also an American, who happened to have been a retired admiral. Like Italy, the Organization of African Unity expressed misgivings concerning UN military command, in particular the tactics and interpretation of the peacekeeping mandate. The situation in Somalia at the time of UNOSOM II's takeover from UNITAF in May 1993 was one in which "humanitarian assistance was reaching those who needed it, but serious security problems remained because of the availability of large quantities of arms, the lack of state structures, and chronic power struggles" (Makinda 1993, p. 185).

Not surprisingly, a lot of criticism has come from a number of camps, most vociferously — but certainly not exclusively — from Somalis and members of the NGO community, who argued that the Secretary-General had increasingly favoured military and security objectives at the expense of all others. This was amplified for both the UN development community and NGOs in Somalia in September 1993, when 50 "crack US Ranger troops" in search of General Aideed stormed a UN compound in Mogadishu and manhandled UN staff and looted the premises of a United Nations Development Programme (UNDP) office (*Toronto Star*, 1 and 5 September 1993). In July 1993, 20 relief NGOs pleaded with the UN to put more resources into the delivery of food and other humanitarian aid — 725 tonnes of food aid had been left to rot at the port because of a lack of military escort outside Mogadishu (Globe and Mail 1993). In July 1993, Jan Eliasson, the UN Undersecretary-General for Humanitarian Affairs, observed that the international community "was spending ten dollars on military protection for every dollar of humanitarian assistance" and that "unless sufficient funds are provided for rehabilitation activities, there is a risk that the military operation can be perceived as an end in itself" (Eliasson 1993, cited in Makinda 1993, p. 185). The same point was made by Sahnoun (1994a), who argued that peacekeeping costs in Somalia "dwarfed" humanitarian-aid costs. By his estimation, it cost US $2 billion in peacekeeping to deliver US $50 million of humanitarian assistance (Sahnoun 1994a).

A mission for peace is weakened when the scope of its activities is narrowed. If a mission becomes so deeply embroiled in the security or military dimensions of a conflict as to be unable to pursue activities in the political or socioeconomic arenas, it ceases to be a mission for peace. Although the relative emphasis on the individual components that make up a mission will depend on the nature of the conflict, a balance needs to be struck among mission activities. In Somalia, the military objectives of the US-dominated UNITAF and UNOSOM II mission have been criticized for overshadowing the broader objectives. The skewed allocation of resources reflected the imbalance of the mission.

The emphasis on the military-security dimensions of a conflict, whether real or merely perceived, inevitably evokes accusations of bias, particularly from local communities. Thus, in the Somalia case, some commentators suggest that, as Jana (1993, p. 29) put it, "the international community has become an instrument of United States foreign policy" and that "the language of the Security Council has become so bellicose that it makes the UN appear not as an instrument of peace but rather a tool of militarism." Accusations of bias, however, are not directed only toward foreign military actors in Somalia. Some have argued that the tragedy in Somalia has led to philanthropic imperialism, whereby relief agencies wield extraordinary power in war-ravaged Third World countries where the authority of governments has disintegrated (de Waal and Omaar 1993). As the conflict continues, international commitment wanes, and initial supporters like France, Italy, and the United States have disentangled themselves.

In general, people have tended to focus rather myopically on the peacekeeping components of missions for peace. With this tendency comes a danger that peacekeeping may be confused with, or substituted for, the other two processes. However, peacekeeping, in the absence of peacemaking and peacebuilding, succeeds only in imposing an armed peace, and the removal of peacekeeping troops invites a return to the status quo ante. Thus, although peacekeeping may contribute to the management of a conflict (by inhibiting overt violence), on its own it does not facilitate resolution. Indeed, peacekeeping may inhibit parties from moving toward peaceful accommodation by isolating the two communities, freezing an unsettled status quo, and rigidifying the boundaries between groups.

One theoretical position (with which I am uncomfortable) that would sustain this argument was developed by Zartman (1985). He asserted that a conflict is "ripe for resolution" when it reaches a "hurting stalemate" — a flare-up in hostilities followed by a "grinding crisis" and deadlock, in which neither side is able to achieve its aims unilaterally, no possibility of escalating or winning exists, and both sides realize the unacceptable costs of being locked in a violent dead end. Thus, the intervention of peacekeepers may effectively subsidize the level of violence and thereby perpetuate the conflict by not allowing it to get worse so that it can get better.

One may take quite a different (and morally less questionable) tack and argue that the imposition of peacekeepers and subsequent limiting of constructive contact between groups may also inhibit the "ripening" process. If "all peacebuilding strategies involve greater interparty contact" (Ryan 1990, p. 61), then peacekeeping inhibits peacebuilding to the extent that it inhibits interparty contact. Peacekeeping and peacebuilding are antithetical processes applied to different groups in a conflict. As Ryan (1990, p. 61) also pointed out, "whereas peacekeeping is about building barriers between the warriors, peacebuilding tries to build bridges between the ordinary people."

In the Somalia case, the peacekeeping mission was transformed into a peace-enforcement mission — new and uncharted territory for the UN. The more cut-and-dried implications of traditional peacekeeping operations are less clear in this new form of activity. In Somalia, it appears to have facilitated the short-term humanitarian objectives of the mission (the delivery of food and humanitarian aid) but to have hindered long-term political, economic, and social objectives.

One of the reasons that the initial mission for peace in Somalia was transformed into an armed humanitarian intervention was the mistaken belief that a military solution could be applied to both military and nonmilitary problems. According to MacKenzie (1994), military analysts believed that Somalia was

> *beautifully set up for a military operation. Someone had conveniently put the capital on the Indian Ocean, so you could do an amphibious operation. You could secure the capital and expand out. You had good fields of vision — soldiers like to see as far as they possibly can. Security was relatively easy. And so the world said, "Lets do something in Somalia."*

The fatal flaw with this logic is that it conceives of the Somalia crisis in strictly military terms. However, the military dimension is but one dimension of the conflict. A solution that considers only the violent manifestations of conflict is doomed to fail because it neglects the social, economic, and political dimensions that buttress and sustain such violence. In future deliberations on whether and how to participate in a large-scale mission for peace, we will need to fit each of these pieces into a common understanding of the nature of the conflict and, relatedly, the nature of an appropriate collective response.

The military-backed humanitarian operation in Somalia received crucial impetus from the Bush Administration in Washington. With a US election in the air, Somalia was seen as a convenient way of winning some votes. The American planners expected to jump into Somalia, "stabilize the military situation," and hand the matter back to the UN within 3 or 4 months (Bolton 1994, p. 58). The case of Somalia points to the tension between short-term political needs and long-term requirements for peace and development. One sees an increasingly conspicuous dissonance between the short cycles of electoral politics in donor countries and the longer time frame needed for missions for peace to show results. Because building peace is typically slow and low key, it does not fit well into the short-term domestic political agendas of politicians in the North. Short-term humanitarian relief programs conducted at the expense of longer term development programs may succeed only in meeting the domestic requirements of politicians in the North while conveniently generating many more opportunities for high-profile interventions; the fundamental structures of underdevelopment and conflict will be untouched, and the prospects for peace are reduced.

Learning the Right Lessons and Building on Hidden Successes

Assessments of international intervention tend to focus on state actors and the military aspects of the operation. However, it is important to also recognize, and learn from, some of the nonmilitary initiatives undertaken by nonstate actors. Future initiatives must integrate the military and nonmilitary dimensions of intervention if the chances of success are to be increased. The following subsections present a number of suggestions for facilitating this process.

NGOs in the peacebuilding process

NGOs are essential actors in missions for peace. In addition to being intimately familiar with the social, political, and economic context in which peacebuilding must be undertaken, NGOs possess a wealth of hands-on, local-level expertise that may be applicable to the peacebuilding process (for example, experience with infrastructural-development, education, cooperative, and cooperation projects). Just as important is the fact that NGOs are located in the interstice between societal and state actors and therefore occupy a strategically important position in conflict situations. In the case of El Salvador, for instance, "the presence of NGOs in the polarized context of civil war established a kind of mediation between the unsatisfied needs of the population and the social and economic policies of successive governments" (Solis and Martin 1992, p. 104).

It is also important to recognize the peacebuilding contributions of NGOs whose projects are not conventionally viewed as being peace related. NGOs with projects in agriculture, irrigation, health, education, urban-poverty alleviation, and so on often find themselves quite literally on the front lines of violent conflict. Realistically, NGO activities alone cannot resolve the protracted social conflicts so prevalent in the world today. However, NGOs possess the underappreciated potential to significantly contribute to conflict management and resolution in those areas in which they have direct experience. Nevertheless, their activities also have the potential to exacerbate tensions and inhibit conflict management (see, for example, Gillies 1992). The capacity of NGOs to influence events must be carefully evaluated because it may vary considerably from case to case. NGOs might also play an important role in monitoring, early warnings, and informed debate on issues surrounding involvement in peace initiatives (both missions for peace and the smaller scale initiatives). Clearly, such a role would be undertaken only if it did not jeopardize their ability to carry out their primary development functions (for example, by politicizing their organization and activities); and they have the resources to undertake this role (so that they would not need to redirect existing resources and weaken current activities).

Support for indigenous peace efforts

In Somalia, a disjuncture has developed between legitimacy, authority, and power. The power of the gun has consolidated the coercive authority of warlords and displaced the more traditional and legitimate system based on discussion and compromise. However, warlordism has not erased traditional forms of social and political relations. Two noteworthy initiatives provide useful examples of how external actors may encourage a process that pushes gun-based power to the margins by recentring traditional sources of social relations. Encouraging these types of initiatives in the context of a multifaceted mission for peace would help to integrate bottom-up and bottom-down processes.

The first initiative, the Borama and Sanaag elders' conferences, was nurtured by the Mennonite Central Committee Canada (MCCC). I say "nurtured" because, although the MCCC and other external NGOs helped to finance the conference (for a total cost of US $100 000), they did not play a direct role in the deliberations (Hiebert and Epp 1993; Omaar 1994). These meetings, in early 1993, brought together hundreds of Somali elders and thousands of advisers for a period of almost 5 months. This national conference was the culmination of a series of multilateral conferences at the regional level, which were themselves the culmination of a series of bilateral peace conferences. After this period of extended discussion, the elders and advisers arrived at a consensus on how to govern Somaliland and how to resolve interclan conflicts. Specifically, the conference adopted a country-wide security framework, laid down a national constitutional structure, and enabled a peaceful change in government (Omaar 1994). Although this initiative marked the beginning of a solution, rather than a solution per se, it was most notable for its support of an indigenous Somali peace effort and its willingness to use indigenous methods of conflict management.

The second initiative was the process leading up to the signing of the Hiraab Treaty in January 1994, an eight-point peace agreement reached by 310 delegates from five Hawiye clans. The fact that this was a direct treaty between clans, rather than between their politicians or military leaders, is seen as being very significant for other peace efforts. If the treaty holds, it would serve to demonstrate the peacemaking expertise inherent in the Somali indigenous social system.

The MCCC makes it clear (see Hiebert and Epp 1993, p. 11) that if these types of approaches are to work, members of the international community must have

- A long-term commitment to nurturing indigenous conflict-management structures and processes;
- a "thorough understanding of, and sensitivity to, cultural factors relevant to conflict resolution"; and
- A willingness to build "a relationship of trust between [internal–indigenous] partners, based on significant and long-term involvement in the country."

Building the political space in which indigenous groups can work out their own solutions to their problems is not a quick or easy process. However, if solutions are to be sustainable, the effort to build this political space may ultimately be the crucial ingredient in a successful mission for peace.

This type of innovative, bottom-up conflict-resolution strategy need not — indeed, should not — be adopted in isolation from other efforts at other levels involving other actors. In other words, a multi-track approach is likely the most productive course of action. However, a multitrack approach may entail coordination problems and the danger that parallel efforts may jump the track and stymie the overall mission for peace. But these problems can be reduced if they are anticipated.

Early action and prevention

The international community is still driven by a reactive logic. However, we should be putting an equal emphasis on preventive action. If the fundamental sources of conflict and underdevelopment lie within a country's internal political, economic, and social structures, then development assistance should contribute to changing those structures. This requires extremely delicate political balancing. For example, some have argued that cutting ODA to repressive regimes is an effective way to effect change. Others — such as Mahbub Huq, special adviser to the UNDP — argue that aid embargoes on countries with poor human-rights records succeed only in hurting the people most in need. Instead, Huq suggests, governments could improve human rights in developing countries by making their aid conditional on cuts in military budgets (Stackhouse 1993). A middle path, suggested by the case of South Africa, would be targeting and channeling aid through local NGOs. However, with this strategy comes the danger of overtly politicizing NGO activity and increasing the risk to NGO workers and their work.

If preventive action is to be effective, we need to nurture and develop an ongoing program to both monitor conflict potential and reinforce peacebuilding capacities in a range of countries and regions. At the moment, the institutions and individuals with the ability to engage in this type of activity tend to work in isolation from one another, and more often than not this expertise has been ineffectively incorporated into policy decision-making processes. However, this may be changing slowly, as reflected in the historic briefing session in February 1997 on the Great Lakes region of Africa, in which for the first time NGOs (CARE USA, OXFAM–UK, and Médecins sans frontières) presented their ideas and assessments directly to the UN Security Council. As NGOs have become increasingly important in the formulation and implementation of policy, international organizations and the state actors involved in them have come to see collaboration as being in their own interest and to rely more and more on NGOs for their ideas, technical understanding, and practical experience. Nonetheless, numerous observers of the Somalia crisis have argued that the reluctance of international actors to respond to NGOs' early warnings of looming catastrophe resulted in a far larger and more costly undertaking than would have been necessary had the reaction been quicker. The genocide in Rwanda reflects the same international failure to respond to clear and unambiguous signals (Adelman et al. 1996; Millwood 1996). The need to connect early warning and early action is as obvious as it is neglected.

Coordination and integration

The international community is slowly learning the right lessons from its experience in both Somalia and Rwanda, particularly the recognition of the need for close cooperation among the various strands of international activity in a humanitarian crisis. The Steering Group for the Multinational Force for Zaire in late 1996 attempted to incorporate these lessons into the development of its mission. As originally conceived, the Steering Group had a mandate not only to provide direction to the military component of the mission but also to ensure coordination of humanitarian, peacebuilding, reconstruction, and political activities in the region and to liaise with the SRSG and the UN Humanitarian Coordinator. Similarly, the Force Commander put in place a small liaison team to advise him on the civilian side of the operation, a team comprising political, humanitarian, legal, and human-rights advisers. However, events in that conflict derailed the full deployment of the multinational force, and these arrangements were never put to the test. It is this type of innovation that deserves further attention as we wrestle with the humanitarian challenges that confront us today.

The post-Cold War world is not as novel as it was in the years immediately following the dissolution of the Soviet Union. A body of international experience with conflicts around the world has been accumulating as international actors attempt to support and strengthen the making, building, and keeping of peace. We have had successes as well as failures, hope as well as frustration. Although each conflict is unique, each also offers generalizable lessons that can be applied elsewhere. The task of learning — and in some cases, relearning — from our experience requires us to critically examine our successes as well as our failures. We need to ask ourselves not only "What lessons have we learned from cases like Mozambique and Somalia?" but also "What lessons should we learn from them?" As we attempt to draw lessons from recent experiences, we should recognize that the cost of this learning process is borne overwhelmingly by the children, women, and men in war-torn societies.

Chapter 5

Conclusion

Linking peace and development

Gregory Wirick and Robert Miller

The three preceding case studies all deal with intrastate conflict: they concern countries in the throes of civil war and the effects that different kinds of outside interventions have had on the course of those wars. These case studies exemplify the types of conflicts most prevalent in the post-Cold War era, although the Gulf War reminds us that conflicts between states are not a thing of the past. Nonetheless, as the world heads into the 21st century, the leading conflicts are likely to be governance related and to have their roots in the dissolution of the colonial empires of the last century.

What lessons are to be learned from the case studies? What implications do they have for the theory and practice of missions for peace, particularly as practiced by Canada? These are the questions to which we now turn.

As we noted in the Introduction, these case studies all warn us about the constraints and sheer bloody difficulties that confront the international community when it decides to intervene in the affairs of countries rent by conflict. Each of the papers focuses on a different aspect of the constraints operating on missions for peace. In the paper on Nicaragua, Andrés Pérez dealt with the legacies of history. Gérard Hervouët, in the paper on Cambodia, stressed the role of foreign policy; and in the paper on Somalia, Kenneth Bush analyzed the organizational and managerial "anarchies" that accompany missions for peace.

Each of the case studies focused on a period that is now several years old, but recent events only deepen our sense of the limitations and complexities that attend these international interventions. Nicaragua remains sunk in an economic depression that grinds down the majority of the people and maintains the potential for conflict. It cannot be said that the time since the end of the civil war has been seized by the elites of Nicaragua to "begin to construct a minimum social consensus as the foundation of a durable peace," to quote the modest hope expressed by Professor Pérez (this volume, p. 47). In the case of Cambodia, recent events have revealed the shallowness of the political accommodation between opposing factions brokered by the United Nations (UN). Faced with the apparent emergence of strongman rule, the international community is now grappling with the question of whether to disengage from Cambodia. Finally, recent events concerning Canada's participation in the UN operation in Somalia have provided bitter lessons for Canadians. In documenting cases of torture and murder by Canadian peacekeepers, the Royal Commission on Somalia has raised doubts in the minds of Canadians about their country's involvement in such missions.

Nonetheless, it would be a misreading of the case studies to conclude that they are arguments against missions for peace. On the contrary, all three spring from a conviction that such missions can be strengthened by developing a better understanding of the basic forces at work in such operations. We will underline this point by taking a closer look at the arguments presented by our three authors.

NICARAGUA: HISTORICAL SPACE AND NATIONAL CONSENSUS

History is a succession of self-reinforcing events conforming to recurring tendencies. For much of Nicaragua's modern history, the events add up to a repeated lesson in the limitations of national power. Successive Nicaraguan governments have adopted policies based on the importance of catering first to the United States and then to the Soviet Union. With such uncertain sovereignty, political polarization became the rule, with the aim being to satisfy allies abroad, not to build consensus at home.

Pérez highlighted the critical importance of sovereignty as a prerequisite to establishing effective governance and thus peace. In his analysis, the "centroamericanization" of the peace process had two important results. It brought about a recognition of the commonality and interconnectedness of the factors giving rise to conflict throughout much of Central America, and even more importantly it "imposed more direct responsibility for the outcome of the [peace] negotiations on the governments of the region" (Pérez, this volume, p. 37). The latter effect went to the heart of the problem of empty sovereignty, an important legacy of Central American history.

The peace process created what Pérez (this volume, p. 23) called "new historical opportunities" (what we have chosen to call historical space) for contending forces within Nicaragua. Like a firebreak in a forest fire, this space created a temporary opportunity to contain destructive forces. However, it did not generate a new consensus, nor could it, for reasons that Pérez (this volume, p. 42) went on to explain:

> *It was not a process whereby power contenders reached some fundamental agreements regarding the organization of the social, political, and economic life of the country. Peace in Nicaragua was simply a stop to the war, forced by external conditions that made it impossible for the Sandinistas and the Contras to continue their military confrontation. The success of the mission for peace in Nicaragua was not based on its capacity to bring the power contenders to an agreement about the future of the country; rather, the mission for peace succeeded because of its capacity to use the opportunities created by the end of the Cold War to officialize an* alto al fuego *(cease-fire).*

This conclusion does not in any way invalidate the mission for peace in Central America; it merely highlights its limitations. It brings home to us that all the terms associated with missions for peace — including peacekeeping, peacemaking, and peacebuilding — are in a sense misnomers. None is a condition of peace; rather, all are at best preconditions that will come to naught unless a genuine indigenous process of building a "minimum social consensus" begins to occur. Without that, missions for peace are likely to be only postponements of war.

What, then, are the prospects for building social consensus? And what is the role of the international community in that process? Here the argument presented by Pérez raises major issues for Canadian policy and donor policy generally. He argued that the grounds on which consensus can be built have been greatly reduced by the global imposition of a liberal-democratic model that severely constrains the role of the state. This "reduces the possibility of using state power as an effective instrument for the articulation of a social consensus on the future of Nicaraguan society" (Pérez, this volume, p. 43). In turn, with this diminution of the role of the state, the object of political conflict may be displaced onto civil society, thus intensifying political fragmentation and creating conditions for "a war of all against all."

In the age of revolution, conflicts were typically between political groups divided ideologically over the uses of state power. Conflicts today are much more likely to be intergroup disputes within society, with the role of the state and political programs relegated to the status of afterthoughts. This might seem like six of one misery in place of a half dozen of the other, but the more anomic nature of conflict poses special problems for the creation of any consensus to serve as the foundation of lasting peace. In particular, the state is likely to be so weak that it is unable to reinforce a consensus with effective and authoritative policies. Contending parties then have little or no confidence that agreements will be respected or enforced. In consequence, these conflicts tend toward the most extreme outcomes, such as genocide, expulsion, or partition.

In considering the role of outside actors in building social consensus, we must bring fundamental issues of governance much closer to our centre of attention. The downsizing of the state has been approached by international financial institutions and donors as if it were an issue exclusively of economic efficiency and management. In fact, the state supplies some of the essential glue holding society together. We are encouraged by recent indications that the role of the state is being freshly reappraised. In *World Development Report 1997: The State in a Changing World*, the World Bank (1997) repeated its familiar argument in favour of state withdrawal from many areas of economic regulation and activity. However, the World Bank also argued that the state has an essential role to play in development and that without an effective state, development will be greatly impaired. Pérez's paper contributed to the reappraisal of the role of the state by highlighting its function in building social consensus.

Finally, we turn to the role of Canada in the Nicaraguan peace process. Professor Pérez described Canada's role as being useful and important at two levels: at the technical level, Canada played a role in verification of agreements; and at the political level, Canada played a role in supporting the people directly engaged in the negotiation and implementation of the agreements. In the latter role, Canada helped to expand the political space in which the initiatives evolved "by actively promoting an interpretation of the sources, nature, and implications of the Central American crisis that was significantly different from that of the United States" (Pérez, this volume, p. 44). In particular, Canada advanced a multidimensional view of the roots of the crisis, in contrast to the unidimensional Cold War vision put forward by the US government. By so doing, Canada supported "the solution of internal political, economic and social problems by the countries and peoples of the region themselves" (Charland 1984, p. 4).

In praising the Canadian contribution, Pérez dissented from the view that the consolidation of peace can be effected by peacebuilding, which he described as "highly desirable but impractical" (Pérez, this volume, p. 45). This conclusion follows from his argument that missions for peace can create a window of opportunity for a country in crisis but that the power contenders in that country must then convert that opportunity into sustainable peace. Barring that, peacebuilding is bound to be ineffectual, no matter how well intentioned. He concluded by suggesting that the most that Canada can or should do in the post-conflict situation is to create a "neutral forum for continuous dialogue among the affected country's political contenders" (Pérez, this volume, p. 46).

This analysis provides a compelling and consistent argument in favour of recognizing the limits of intervention and the need to return power as quickly and completely as possible to the local contenders. If this is not done, missions for peace might only perpetuate the conditions giving rise to conflict, particularly the absence of political sovereignty and consequent failure to develop a national political consensus. Clientalism will have been preserved — only the names of the patrons will have changed.

Cambodia: The Role of Foreign Policy

Missions for peace take place in the intersection where international relations meet local history. Professor Hervouët's analysis of the Cambodian case serves as a powerful reminder of that fact. The Cambodian peace process, like the Central American one, was affected by changes taking place in the Soviet Union under then President Gorbachev. His government set out to improve relations with China, and as a consequence the intransigence of both the Chinese and the Vietnamese regarding a peace settlement in Cambodia began to soften. These changes in the international environment quickly made their influence felt by the Cambodian factions, who began to show a new willingness to negotiate.

In broad outline, the Nicaraguan and Cambodian missions for peace illustrate how the end of the Cold War positively affected the settlement of Third World conflicts, and they remind us of the corrosive effects of the Cold War in many parts of the world. As in Central America, the regional powers in Cambodia played an important role in the peace process, but this role was secondary to that of the five permanent members of the Security Council.

The story of Canada's involvement in the Cambodian mission for peace belies the usual depiction of Canada as the international boy scout, always willing to volunteer and to set no limits to its commitments. Indeed, Hervouët documented both the caution with which Canada approached involvement in the Cambodian mission for peace and the role that ulterior foreign-policy interests played in Canada's eventual willingness to become involved. Canada's experience with the International Commissions for Control and Supervision in Cambodia, Laos, and Viet Nam had "profoundly marked the collective memory of Canadian diplomacy" (Hervouët, this volume, p. 52), creating a strong desire at the Department of External Affairs to steer clear of regional-security entanglements. Even with the emergence of new Canadian foreign-policy interests, notably in human rights, trade, and investment, this aversion was slow to dissipate. For a time, Canada hoped it would be possible to build closer commercial and political ties while keeping its distance on security issues, but as Hervouët (this volume, p. 56) noted,

> *It was becoming increasingly difficult to explain, often within the same documents and speeches, that Asia and the Pacific were henceforth more important economically to Canada than Europe, that Asian immigration exceeded that from European sources, but that the federal government remained firmly committed to its traditionally cautious stance on regional-security matters.*

It is worth pausing for a moment to reflect on this point because it is often argued that trade and commercial interests can in effect diminish or even cancel out other foreign-policy interests, and there are obviously examples of this. But in the Cambodian case, those same commercial interests motivated the Canadian foreign-policy establishment, somewhat reluctantly, to deepen its involvement in regional-security and development issues in Southeast Asia. This suggests that the relationship between trade and other elements of foreign policy is more complex than is sometimes acknowledged. As the concept of security broadens, it becomes increasingly difficult to maintain a unidimensional foreign-policy relationship with any part of the world.

Eventually making the decision to engage security issues in its relations with Southeast Asia, Canada nevertheless continued to play its hand very cautiously, indeed timidly, in Hervouët's estimation. It lobbied successfully to participate in the Paris Conference but then disappointed the UN with the modesty of its contribution to the United Nations Transnational Authority in Cambodia (UNTAC) missions. Canadians played a very useful technical role throughout the process but avoided proposing policy solutions, preferring the role of helpful fixer to that of foreign-policy architect. All of this is at odds with the common portrait of Canadians as wide-eyed innocents, eager to rush in where angels fear to tread. In Cambodia, Canada has trod very carefully indeed.

In contrast to the modesty of the Canadian role, the UN mission for peace in Cambodia was breathtakingly ambitious. As Hervouët noted, it was a UN operation of unprecedented complexity that "went well beyond peacekeeping to encompass an ambitious attempt to re-create, in the space of a short mandate, the political, economic, and social conditions of a society torn by deep-rooted antagonisms ever since the US intervention in the Viet Nam war" (Hervouët, this volume, p. 69). In short, UNTAC set for itself precisely the sort of goals that Peréz warned against in his case study of Nicaragua. Why, despite similar foreign-policy constraints, did the Cambodian mission for peace go so much further than the one in Nicaragua?

The explanation is to be found in the critical difference between a country seriously damaged by conflict and another devastated by it. The Nicaraguan civil war dragged on for the better part of a generation and inflicted very serious economic and social damage; nonetheless, at the end of the war, many of the country's institutions were more or less intact and one could imagine an internal process of reconstruction, provided the contending parties would allow that to happen. By contrast, during that same period, Cambodia was entangled in the Viet Nam war, suffered unimaginably through a holocaust, and finally wound up under foreign military occupation. The end result in Cambodia was a society in which human capital had been decimated and, in consequence, one in which institutions had effectively disappeared. If the problem in Nicaragua was a lack of a will for peace, the problem in Cambodia was one of missing capacity. This small country was not a failed state but a state destroyed.

In the circumstances, the international community had no choice but to give a broad mandate to the Cambodian mission for peace. The social, economic, and political infrastructure that would have allowed the country to resume its life after the cessation of the conflict simply did not exist. Much of it had to be rebuilt and sustained with international assistance. Accordingly, we would amend the prescription offered by Peréz, who wrote that missions for peace should try to meet their twin objectives — that is, ending conflict and creating windows of opportunity for sustainable peace — with the minimum necessary intervention and should engage indigenous actors as completely and quickly as possible. However, we would add that the depth and duration of intervention must vary, depending on the needs and circumstances of the country. Where missions for peace are concerned, there is no "one size that fits all."

Somalia: Anarchies and Missions for Peace

The case studies of Nicaragua and Cambodia highlighted local history and international politics as powerful influences on whether and how missions for peace take place. In the case study of Somalia, Bush focused on the operation itself and, in particular, its mission. His argument, in a nutshell, was that the Somalia operation failed in the end because its mission was defined too narrowly in military terms, thus neglecting other resources, both local and international, that might have helped to resolve the conflict.

Bush began the case study by describing what he regards as the unique characteristic of missions for peace, namely, that they are multidimensional. Typically, they contain activities from all of the elements (peacekeeping, peacemaking, preventive diplomacy, and peacebuilding) in Boutros-Ghali's (1992) *An Agenda for Peace*, and these activities are carried out by a wide variety of actors, including government, nongovernmental organzations (NGOs), and private and multinational organizations. In this perspective, the success of the mission depends mainly on how these various activities and actors fit together (Bush, this volume, p. 83):

> *A central idea in a mission for peace is that the success of a peace initiative is more than the sum of the separate impacts of each of these activities. Success depends on the ways the different components of these types of intervention mesh with each other and (as importantly) with existing social, political, and economic structures in war-torn societies.*

According to Bush, the failure of the mission in Somalia was rooted in the evolution of the country's crisis and the subsequent international response. In the decade or so before the UN intervention, Somalia gradually descended into a clan-dominated, militaristic anarchy. In time, this anarchy took the form of marauding militias in which power was wielded primarily by warlords and their gunmen. The consequences for effective governance were severe, as both central political institutions and traditional, clan-based authority structures withered and disappeared. In addition, fire power possessed by these gangs escalated ominously, giving them the capacity to destroy the basic infrastructure of the country in a relatively short period of time. This devastation, combined with the severe drought in late 1991, created the perfect conditions for a human catastrophe. By March 1992, the International Committee of the Red Cross estimated that one-third of the Somali population, or about 1.5 million people, were at serious risk of death from starvation over a 6-month period.

As the case study shows, the international community was slow to respond, but when it eventually responded, it did so on a large scale and militarily. The international response was heavily conditioned by public pressure on Western governments that was engendered by media coverage of the famine. That pressure eventually led the Security Council to mount a large-scale humanitarian intervention, rather than support the gradual approach taken by Mohamed Sahnoun, the Secretary-General's Special Representative in Somalia. Sahnoun was attempting to reach a political settlement through existing social and political structures to, as Professor Bush (this volume, p. 96) described it, "modify those very same structures."

The decision to intervene heavily had immediately positive results, namely, the opening of supply routes for the delivery of humanitarian aid and the mitigation of terrible suffering. The presence of US-led peacekeepers with a mandate to "make" peace contained the warring factions for a time but did little or nothing to resolve the underlying conflict. In fact, peacekeeping may well have inhibited parties from moving toward peaceful accommodation "by isolating the two communities, freezing an unsettled status quo, and rigidifying the boundaries between groups" (Bush, this volume, p. 103). This dynamic, in turn, led to frequent violent incidents between peacekeepers and Somalis and the eventual abandonment of the mission.

It is impossible to say whether the approach of Mohamed Sahnoun would have worked, given the power of the local warlords and the atrophy of traditional political structures. Nonetheless, the Somalian case study highlights the point made earlier by Pérez that international intervention should be seen as only a window for peace and not as peace itself. For humanitarian reasons, the international community may well have to intervene extensively in situations like Somalia, but somehow the path of engaging and empowering local political forces and communities must be followed at the same time. Realism forces us to concede that balancing these two opposing requirements will be enormously difficult, because although peacebuilding demands dialogue and engagement with local forces, humanitarian intervention will, in all probability, lead to confrontation and conflict. Clearly, missions for peace are delicate, complex political operations requiring careful coordination of different, sometimes divergent, elements.

In Bush's judgment, the mission for peace in Somalia failed most conspicuously in the coordination of diverse elements. By concentrating on the supposedly quick fix of a military intervention, the mission neglected and then compounded the underlying social, economic, and political crisis in the country. Resources other than the military, such as development NGOs, were underappreciated and underused. At the same time, "the squabbling and turf fights among and between UN and non-UN actors in Somalia became increasingly public as the operation expanded in size and scope" (Bush, this volume, p. 93). These elements of the case study led Bush to characterize the mission in Somalia as the meeting of two anarchies: the local anarchy of clan conflict and the international anarchy of UN intervention. As the author argued, however, each of the operational failures sprang from a deeper cause, namely, the absence of a coherent and realistic sense of mission. Beyond the short-term imperatives of television news and electoral politics, Somalia was a mission for peace without a clear mission.

Lessons learned

In undertakings as complex as missions for peace, we cannot expect simple solutions. Nonetheless, lessons relevant to policy can be found, and we will highlight two of these lessons in this section.

Caution regarding the UN

One lesson concerns the capability of the UN to control and conduct missions for peace. The case studies in this volume suggest that the jury is still out on this matter. As Jan (1996, p. 8) noted recently in regard to the successive UN missions in Somalia,

> *There was never a transition from a military to a civilian emphasis. The military mindset that had guided UNITAF [UN Unified Task Force] continued into UNOSOM II [Second United Nations Operation in Somalia] which should have essentially been a civilian operation ... .*

Apart from the mission's short-run humanitarian value, it was a failure.

In Cambodia, on the other hand, as Hervouët made clear, the UN achieved some of its objectives. Yet here, too, quite substantial criticisms have been made. A number of important opportunities to build an enduring peace were missed during the UNTAC period. Many Cambodians, whose expectations had soared during the economic boomlet of the UNTAC period, were sorely disappointed in the aftermath and are now bitter and cynical about the UN's brief but seminal role in shaping their country's future. "The sudden influx of international agencies, foreign personnel, and external aid led to fairly high rates of economic growth, but also to a growth process that was extremely skewed" (Utting 1994, p. 9). The boom took place almost exclusively in the capital of Phnom Penh and was chiefly confined to the service sector that catered to foreign residents and organizations. The fact is that "rehabilitation was a marginal facet of the UNTAC operation" (Utting 1994, p. 27); some argued that certain socioeconomic characteristics emerged during the peace process that have had negative consequences for the country's rehabilitation and development.

The reality is that multilateral interventions through the UN are bound to be extremely intricate undertakings, with very delicate political components. This makes them prone to contradiction, confusion, and even chaos and, arguably, more prone to serious setbacks than a unilateral intervention would be. In his paper on Somalia, Bush quoted Canadian Major General Lewis MacKenzie as concluding that UN operations are always conducted with less than what they need, whereas subcontractual missions — like UNITAF — invariably have more than they need. As Bush rightly pointed out, this makes Canadian soldiers more vulnerable in UN operations than in coalition missions.

Canada should face this problem squarely by no longer assuming that the UN is the be-all and end-all of our multilateral involvements in security and development. UN requests for support should be examined on their merits, before considerations of multilateral solidarity are taken into account. NATO is an obvious alternative in the security sphere and could be teamed with the Organization for Security and Co-operation in Europe to provide civilian skills in a complex mission. Other regional organizations — with or without Canada's participation — should be encouraged to take the lead in resolving crises within their regions.

A related policy issue is whether a multitude of contributing nations can form a coherent and effective force if many of the troops or civilians are ill-acquainted with the country they have been sent to. The customs and practices among disparate militaries and civilians from various countries make the creation of an esprit de corps exceedingly difficult, especially when people are under huge pressure to perform rapidly, produce results, and finish the job. To overcome these built-in difficulties, the leadership must be exceptional and the circumstances highly favourable.

A rapid-reaction force at the disposal of the Secretary-General would undoubtedly be a better approach. As noted earlier, Foreign Affairs Minister Axworthy has also raised the possibility of civilian rapid-response teams. However, the political obstacles facing such proposals would probably be insurmountable in the next 10 years, owing to the suspicions of a highly nationalistic US Congress. In the meantime, Canada should be wary of participating in large and unwieldy UN missions. Also, the Security Council should become more selective in its engagements, something that is already happening. The willingness to engage in a plethora of missions during the early years of the 1990s has been replaced by a much more prudent approach (Findlay 1995, pp. 69–70):

> *The UN and contributor states are obliged to weigh competing resources in deciding where to invest their limited resources. This will involve essentially abandoning some states to their own devices when, despite best endeavours, the international community appears unable appreciably to affect political outcomes. Somalia has come to epitomize this dawning realization.*

The persistence of conflict

At a peacebuilding seminar in Geneva sponsored by the UN Research Institute for Social Development (UNRISD), it was noted that "the end of armed conflict rarely signifies the resolution of conflict" (UNRISD 1994, p. 6). One should assume that the factors militating against a successful (that is, peaceful) outcome normally outweigh those favouring peace. This is explained by the chaos that descends upon societies in conflict, the confusion that often accompanies efforts to help, and the enormous obstacles outsiders face in seeking to comprehend and influence the situation. For this reason, the Canadian Policy Roundtable identified internal order and security as one of three broad requirements for action, the others being evolving representative political processes and economic and social reconstruction. Together these three objectives were seen as responding to "the human security needs of war-torn societies" (GOC 1996, p. 6).

In contrast to these complex, long-term requirements, international peacekeeping missions tend to underestimate the time it takes to make the transition from war to peace. UNRISD (1994, p. 7) cautioned that

> *Peace missions need to be formed with the real needs of the country in mind. ... Peace missions enter a country with large numbers of military and civilian staff and become deeply involved in the operation of national institutions and the creation of new security arrangements for a relatively brief period of time. The massive departure of these forces, just as their massive entry, exacerbates problems.*

We are concerned that the Canadian government seems locked into a fast-entry–fast-exit approach. The Foreign Affairs Minister and government documents refer to a window of opportunity, which, by implication, suddenly slams shut and then remains closed (GOC 1996, p. 3):

> *The Canadian ... external initiatives will be short-term. Such policy initiatives will be implemented during the window of opportunity, typically from 24 to 36 months, that exists during negotiations to end a conflict and the associated cessation of hostilities.*

Yet the same document admitted that "one to two years is not a sufficient period of time for complex political restructuring to take root" (GOC 1996, p. 7). Such considerations are particularly relevant to peacebuilding, which requires longer and deeper commitment from outside than other types of mission for peace.

To emphasize this point, it would be worthwhile to rethink the metaphors that have thus far been used to describe the functions of peacebuilding. The language of peacebuilding has been excessively mechanistic and technocratic. Building, constructing, and engineering — with plenty of tools at hand — are the favoured metaphors. All of these metaphors imply imposing something on the landscape, erecting a structure based on the mores of developed countries, and leaving once this rather superficial work is complete. Unintentionally, the language evokes a sense of hubris — "we can easily go in there and sort things out" — when the realities are more likely to confound and confuse.

A subtler approach would be one in which the operative verbs are *to cultivate* and *to nurture*. Such an approach would serve several purposes. First, it would take account of the facts on the ground or, by extension, the circumstances of the country. The role of nature in the metaphor is akin to the roles of history and geography in the case of society. These are the large forces that peacebuilding must accommodate and with which it must interact. Second, it would convey the sense that patience is a virtue and time an important helper. The processes cannot be rushed. This is not an easy lesson to apply when governments rarely have planning horizons longer than 4 or 5 years and, worse still, when the media demand instantaneous results. But instant solutions, or even 5-year plans, do not conform to the way the world works; nor should peacebuilding be forced to accommodate itself to unrealistic timetables.

A level of trust and confidence has to be created concerning the efficacy of peacebuilding, both among its potential beneficiaries and among the population in contributing nations. This is not easy to engender in war-torn countries emerging from years of conflict, or even in Northern countries like Canada in an era of great cynicism about politics. In the Canadian context, creating trust and support means getting the metaphors right. It is an old lament, but a better job has to be done of communicating broad issues of foreign policy to the general public. When highly complex processes are involved, the only way to convey the message is to use relatively simple metaphors, but ones that ring true. That it takes time to grow a garden is self-evident; likewise, it takes time to promote change in a society.

Recommendations for Policy

What emerges throughout the case studies is the dynamic nature of missions for peace. These interventions do have an impact: they do change the situation, sometimes for better, sometimes for worse. Given this, it is important to offer the Canadian government the following recommendations for policy.

Selective engagement

The first recommendation is that the government seek to limit the number of its engagements abroad but be willing to stay the course in those it chooses. This implies a very deliberate commitment of skills and resources over a fairly long period. It means making careful choices based on a calculus of values and interests, as opposed to reacting suddenly to media hysteria and rushing to join the latest multilateral band-aid operation. It means selecting niches in which Canada's expertise and resources can be especially helpful. It also means refusing to become involved in situations that superficially seem compelling, particularly for humanitarian reasons, but in which the outcome is doubtful or worse. These considerations must be weighed carefully because of the real possibility that things will go wrong and that Canadian soldiers will be placed at risk.

After the government has made its choices and selected its niches, it should have a sense of commitment and a willingness to engage with the people and society of a country. As Bush wrote (this volume, p. 102),

> *A mission for peace is weakened when the scope of its activities is narrowed. If a mission becomes so deeply embroiled in the security or military dimensions of a conflict as to be unable to pursue activities in the political or socioeconomic arenas, it ceases to be a mission for peace. … A balance needs to be struck among mission activities.*

This approach also offers a more realistic assessment of the length of time it would take to help societies achieve a sense of renewal after being smashed and dislocated by civil war. Such an approach requires us to make a long-term investment — even a generation-long commitment — rather than making a short, sharp, surgical effort to restore order and then leaving the conflicted society to its own devices. Choosing a peacebuilding approach would mean more than turning down peace-enforcement missions; it would also mean refusing to become involved in some complex humanitarian emergencies and instead continuing to nurture work we have already begun elsewhere.

We would also recommend that the government become engaged in a mission for peace only if it can demonstrate that the mission would involve a reasonable balance of Canadian values and interests. Canada's involvement in Cambodia was an excellent example of this balance, as Hervouët made clear. Nicaragua and Canada's involvement in the Central American peace process would also meet fairly basic criteria for a mission for peace. But Somalia and Rwanda constituted more doubtful cases, largely because the evidence that Canada's interests were at stake was considerably weaker. Common sense must be used in defining interests and values, which is another way of saying that the definitions should be widely shared. There is little point in Canada's becoming significantly involved in countries where its interests are minimal or its values are inimical. There is little point because support within Canada for such an involvement would not be sustained.

Modest expectations

Canada should be modest in its declarations and expectations. Canada may be engaged abroad to effect change, but change can be both good and bad. Canada's involvement gives us so little control of the situation that we should concentrate on deactivating conflict and on planting the seeds of reconciliation and recovery among the population in distress. Some may argue that such an approach is too modest and that bolder goals are needed to galvanize public support. But surely peace must be engendered and nurtured by the people themselves. Peace must be homegrown through local involvement; it cannot be imposed by Canada or any other nation. We should not be there to provide a vision; rather, we should be there to help nurture the vision identified by the people and their leaders. If this vision does not accord with Canadian values, then obviously we should not involve ourselves.

Working groups

Finally, we recommend that Canada encourage the creation of working groups of like-minded donors for specific war-torn societies and be willing to take on a leadership role within certain of these working groups. Canada has many strengths to offer. We have earned a good reputation as peacekeepers. Our conciliation and mediation skills are well developed, and our international network may be one of the best in the world, partly because of the many international "clubs" to which we belong. These resources can help bring adversaries to the table for constructive dialogue and negotiation.

Final words

Former Canadian Prime Minister Lester Pearson often referred to "expanding common ground" as a worthy goal in governance and in life. This sensibility is at the heart of a mission for peace, which is a means of operationalizing the concept of a comprehensive system of conflict prevention and resolution as laid out in *An Agenda for Peace.* For Canada, it also means being prepared to play a significant role in those debates and forums where Canada's interests and values best converge. An editorial in the *Globe and Mail* (1997, p. A18) remarked that "foreign aid and peacekeeping give us stature on the great issues of peace and development." This is a stature that Canada has earned, but the commitment is ongoing and needs to be renewed in spirit and in vigour each year.

Missions for peace offer a framework for policy linking the great issues of peace and development. Their goal is to increase the space for human beings to lead lives untroubled by the disintegrating effects of war and poverty and to join with others in nurturing a civil and civilized society.

Appendix 1

Biographies of Contributing Authors

Gregory Wirick (1952–98) was an Associate with the Parliamentary Centre and Senior Advisor to the Canadian Committee for the Fiftieth Anniversary of the United Nations. Representing the Parliamentary Centre, Mr Wirick acted as Principal Advisor to the Senate Subcommittee on Security and National Defence (1993) and the Special Senate Committee on National Defence (1989). From 1978 to 1982, Mr Wirick was Executive Director of the United Nations Association in Canada. He held an MA from the London School of Economics and was the author of numerous articles on political and diplomatic issues, published in various Canadian media including the *Globe and Mail*, *The Toronto Star*, and *Maclean's*.

Robert Miller is Director of the Parliamentary Centre in Ottawa, Ontario, Canada. His extensive experience in public policy includes parliamentary-strengthening programs abroad and foreign policy reviews in Southern Africa and Southeast Asia. Mr Miller has led numerous studies and published widely in the areas of foreign policy, international development, peacebuilding, human rights, and democratic development. He has taught at the University of the Philippines and the Ateneo de Manila University and traveled widely throughout Asia, Africa, and Latin America.

Andrés Pérez is an Associate Professor in the Department of Political Science at The University of Western Ontario in London, Ontario, Canada. Dr Pérez was formerly the Director of the Nicaraguan Institute of Public Administration and, from 1983 to 1988, a program officer at the International Development Research Centre, where he was responsible for the organization of a multinational research program on participation and public policy.

Gérard Hervouët is a Professor in the Department of Political Science and the Director of the Research and Study Group on Contemporary Asia at Université Laval in Sainte-Foy, Québec, Canada. He is Director of the journal *Études internationales* and serves on the National Defence (Canada) Programme Committee for Military and Strategic Studies, the Grant Selection Committee for the Canada–Asean Centre (Singapore), the Canadian Research Committee for the Humanities for the Asia–Pacific Economic Conference, and the Canadian Committee of the Cooperation and Security Council for the Asia–Pacific Region.

Kenneth Bush is Senior Research Associate with the Peacebuilding and Reconstruction Program Initiative of the International Development Research Centre. He received his PhD in Government from Cornell University (Ithaca, NY, USA) and has held teaching positions at Queen's University and Carleton University in Canada and Bilkent University in Ankara, Turkey. Dr Bush has published widely on issues of peacebuilding, identity-based conflict, and governance.

Appendix 2

Abbreviations and Acronyms

ASEAN	Association of Southeast Asian Nations
CARE	Cooperative for American Relief Everywhere
CFB	Canadian Forces Base
CGDK	Coalition Government of Democratic Kampuchea
CIAV	Comisión Internacional de Apoyo y Verificación (International Commission of Support and Verification)
CIDA	Canadian International Development Agency
CIVS	Comisión Internacional de Verificación y Seguimiento (International Commission for Verification and Follow-up)
CMAC	Cambodian Mine Action Centre
CPP	Cambodian People's Party

FSLN	Frente Sandinista de Liberación Nacional (Sandinista national liberation front)
FUNCINPEC	Front uni national pour un Cambodge indépendant, neutre, pacifique et coopératif (national united front for an independent, neutral, peaceful, and cooperative Cambodia)
GNP	gross national product
ICCS	International Commission for Control and Supervision
ICM	international control mechanism
ICRC	International Committee of the Red Cross
IDRC	International Development Research Centre
MCCC	Mennonite Central Committee Canada
NATO	North Atlantic Treaty Organization
NGO	nongovernmental organization
ODA	official development assistance
ONUCA	United Nations Observer Group in Central America
OXFAM	Oxford Committee for Famine Relief
PACE	Protestant and Catholic Encounter
PLDB	Parti libéral democratique et bouddhiste (Buddhist liberal democratic party) [Cambodia]
PRK	People's Republic of Kampuchea
SNC	Supreme National Council [Cambodia]
SRSG	Special Representative of the Secretary-General [UN]
UN	United Nations
UNAMIC	United Nations Advanced Mission in Cambodia
UNDP	United Nations Development Programme
UNHCR	United Nations High Commission for Refugees
UNICEF	United Nations Children's Fund
UNITAF	United Nations Unified Task Force
UNOSOM I	First United Nations Operation in Somalia
UNOSOM II	Second United Nations Operation in Somalia
UNRISD	United Nations Research Institute for Social Development
UNTAC	United Nations Transitional Authority in Cambodia
WFP	World Food Programme

Bibliography

Acharya, A. 1994. Cambodia, the UN and the problems of peace: an assessment of the United Nations territorial authority in Cambodia. Pacific Review, 7(3), 297–308.

Adelman, H.; Suhrke, A.; Jones, B. 1996. Study 2: Early warning and conflict management: genocide in Rwanda. *In* Millwood, D., ed., The international response to conflict and genocide: lessons from the Rwanda experience. Steering Committee of the Joint Evaluation of Emergency Assistance to Rwanda, Copenhagen, Denmark.

Akashi, Y. 1993. The challenges faced by UNTAC. Japanese Review of International Affairs, 7(3), 185–201.

Alvarez Lejarza, E. 1958. Las constituciones de Nicaragua: exposición, crítica y textos. Ediciones Cultura Hispánica, Madrid, Spain.

Amer, R. 1993. The United Nations' peacekeeping operation in Cambodia: overview and assessment. Contemporary Southeast Asia, 15(2), 211–231.

Anderson, M.B. 1996. Do no harm: supporting local capacities through aid. Local Capacities for Peace Project, The Collaborative for Development Action, Cambridge, MA, USA. 61 pp.

AWC (Africa Watch Committee). 1990. Somalia: a government at war with its own people: testimonies about the killings and the conflict in the north. AWC, New York, NY, USA. 268 pp.

Axworthy, L. 1996. Building peace to last: establishing a Canadian peacebuilding initiative. An address by the Honourable Lloyd Axworthy, Minister of Foreign Affairs, 30 Oct, York University, North York, ON, Canada. Department of Foreign Affairs and International Trade, Ottawa, ON, Canada.

Azar, E.E. 1986. Protracted social conflicts: ten propositions. *In* Azar, E.E.; Burton, J.W., ed., International conflict resolution: theory and practice. Wheatsheaf, Sussex, UK. pp. 28–41.

Barahona, A. 1977. Estudio sobre la historia contemporánea de Nicaragua. Instituto de Investigaciones Sociales, Facultad de Ciencias Sociales, Universidad de Costa Rica. San Pedro de Montes de Oca, San José, Costa Rica. Avance de Investigación No. 24. 62 pp.

Baranyi, S.; North, L. 1992. Stretching the limits of the possible: United Nations peacekeeping in Central America. Canadian Centre for Global Security, Ottawa, ON, Canada. Aurora Papers, No. 15. 59 pp.

Berlin, I. 1992. The bent twig: on the rise of nationalism. *In* Berlin, I., The crooked timber of humanity: chapters in the history of ideas. Vintage Books, New York, NY, USA.

Bermann, K. 1986. Under the big stick: Nicaragua and the United States since 1848. South End Press, Boston, MA, USA. 339 pp.

Bernales, A.O.; Fernandez, R. 1990. Esquipulas II: una tarea pendiente. Editorial Universitaria Centroamericana, San José, Costa Rica.

Bolton, J.R. 1994. Wrong turn in Somalia. Foreign Affairs, 73(1), 56–66.

Boutros-Ghali, B. 1992. An agenda for peace: preventive diplomacy, peacemaking and peacekeeping. United Nations, New York, NY, USA. 48 pp.

——— 1995. Supplement to an agenda for peace; position paper by the Secretary-General on the occasion of the fiftieth anniversary of the United Nations. United Nations, New York, NY, USA. 24 pp.

Bush, K.D 1994. Missions for peace: the case of Somalia. Paper presented at the Missions for Peace Conference, 11 Jul 1994, Parliamentary Centre, Ottawa, ON, Canada.

——— 1995. Towards a balanced approach to rebuilding war-torn societies. Canadian Foreign Policy, 3(3), 49–69.

——— 1996. Beyond bungee cord humanitarianism: towards a *developmental* agenda for peacebuilding. Canadian Journal of Development Studies, 17 (Dec), 75–92.

CARE Canada (Cooperative for American Relief Everywhere). 1993. Annual report. CARE Canada, Ottawa, ON, Canada.

——— 1994. Systems and structures for effective international development and humanitarian relief. A brief prepared for the Special Joint Committee Reviewing Canadian Foreign Policy. CARE Canada, Ottawa, ON, Canada.

Charland, C. 1984. A Canadian view of Latin America and the Caribbean. *In* Canada, the United States, and Latin America: independence and accommodation. Latin American Program, Woodrow Wilson International Center for Scholars, Washington, DC, USA.

Child, J. 1992. The Central American peace process, 1983–1991: sheathing swords, building confidence. Lynne Rienner, Boulder, CO, USA. 200 pp.

CIDA (Canadian International Development Agency) 1994. The role of NGOs in the peacebuilding process. Discussion paper prepared by the NGO Division, Canadian Partnership Branch, CIDA, Ottawa, ON, Canada, Mar. 27 pp.

CIIPS (Canadian Institute for International Peace and Security). 1990. Guide to Canadian policies on arms control, disarmament, defence and conflict resolution. CIIPS, Ottawa, ON, Canada.

Clark, J. 1989a. Canadians face the challenge together: "Pacific 2000." An address by the Hon. Joe Clark, 16 May, Edmonton, AB, Canada. Department of External Affairs, Ottawa, ON, Canada.

——— 1989b. An address by the Hon. Joe Clark, 30 Jul, Paris, France. Department of External Affairs, Ottawa, ON, Canada. Speech No. 89/36.

——— 1990a. Canada and Asia Pacific in the 1990s. An address by the Hon. Joe Clark, Jul, Victoria Chamber of Commerce, Victoria, BC, Canada. Department of External Affairs, Ottawa ON, Canada. Statement No. 90/05.

——— 1990b. Canada and Indochina. A statement by the Hon. Joe Clark, 23 Jan. Department of External Affairs, Ottawa ON, Canada. Statement 90/05.

Cohen, I.J. 1989. Structuration theory: Anthony Giddens and the constitution of social life. Macmillan, London, UK. 307 pp.

Cortés Dominguez, G. 1990. La lucha por el poder. Editorial Vanguardia, Managua, Nicaragua. 394 pp.

Cox, D. 1993. Exploring An Agenda for Peace: issues arising from the report of the Secretary-General. Canadian Centre for Global Security, Ottawa, ON, Canada. Aurora Papers, No. 20. 52 pp.

Cuadra Lira, E. 1997. Gobernalidad y seguridad en Nicaragua: seguridad ciudadana y sus instituciones. Coordinadora Regional de Investigaciones Ecónomicas y Sociales, Managua, Nicaragua.

Delgado Romero, R. 1995. La transición en Nicaragua: gobernalidad, cultura política y opinión pública. Instituto de Estudios Nicaraguenses, Managua, Nicaragua.

DePalma, A. 1997. Canada ponders its peacekeeper role: warriors or watchdogs? The New York Times, 13 Apr, p. 16.

de Waal, A.; Omaar, R. 1993. Doing harm by doing good? The international relief effort in Somalia. Current History, 92(574), 198–202.

DFA (Department of Foreign Affairs). 1993. Canada's response to the crisis in Somalia. DFA, Ottawa, ON, Canada. Update, 4 Oct.

Diederich, B. 1981. Somoza and the legacy of U.S. involvement in Central America. Dutton, New York, NY, USA.

Diehl, P.F. 1993. International peacekeeping. Johns Hopkins University Press, Baltimore, MD, USA. 211 pp.

DiMaggio, P. 1988. Interest and agency in institutional theory. *In* Zucker, L.G., ed., Institutional patterns and organizations: culture and environment. Ballinger, Cambridge, UK. pp. 3–21.

DND (Department of National Defence). 1991a. Canada extends Ethiopian humanitarian relief flights. DND, Ottawa, ON, Canada. News Release No. 45/91, 4 Nov.

——— 1991b. Canadian Forces and Ethiopian humanitarian relief flights. DND, Ottawa, ON, Canada. News Release No. 49/91, 18 Dec.

——— 1992. Press release. DND, Ottawa, ON, Canada. RFN 09/92, 2 Mar.

Dyer, G. 1993. Third World troops take the casualties while West stands back. The Gazette [Montréal], 18 Jun.

EAC (External Affairs Canada). 1989. Press release. EAC, Ottawa, ON, Canada. Press Release No. 72, 5 Apr.

EAITC (External Affairs and International Trade Canada). 1988/89. Annual report 1988–89. EAITC, Ottawa, ON, Canada.

Economist, The. 1993. Who's who? The Economist, 23 Jan, p. 41.

El Semanario. 1996. Comportamiento del suicidio en Nicaragua. El Semanario, 24–30 May, p. 1.

Envío. 1984. Los estados unidos en las elecciones de Nicaragua: tres modelos de intervención. Instituto Histórico Centroamericano, Managua, Nicaragua. Envío, 3(32).

——— 1989. Breakthrough for peace. Instituto Histórico Centroamericano, Managua, Nicaragua. Envío, 8.

Evans, G.J. 1993. Cooperating for peace: the global agenda for the 1990's and beyond. Allen & Unwin Pty Ltd, St Leonards, NSW, Australia. 224 pp.

Findlay, T. 1995. Cambodia: the legacy and lessons of UNCTAC. Oxford University Press, Oxford, UK. Stockholm International Peace Research Institute Research Report No. 9. 238 pp.

Fine, R.; Kruse, D.; Spence, J.; Vickers, G. 1990. Hemisphere initiatives: Nicaragua election update number 2. Foreign funding of the internal opposition. *In* Robinson, W.; MacMichael, D., Intervention in the Nicaraguan election. Cover Action Information Bulletin No. 33.

Frost, F. 1993. The peace process in Cambodia: issues and prospects. Centre for the Study of Australia–Asia Relations, Griffith University, Nathan, Queensland, Australia. CSAAR Australia–Asia Papers, No. 69. 63 pp.

Giddens, A. 1984. The constitution of society: outline of the theory of structuration. University of California Press, Berkeley, CA, USA.

Gillies, D. 1992. Principled intervention: Canadian aid, human rights and the Sri Lankan conflict. *In* Miller, R., ed., Aid as peacemaker: Canadian development assistance and Third World conflict. Carleton University Press, Ottawa, ON, Canada. pp. 33–50.

Gizewski, P.; Pearson, G. 1993. The burgeoning cost of UN peace-keeping: who pays and who benefits? Canadian Centre for Global Security, Ottawa, ON, Canada. Aurora Papers, No. 21. 31 pp.

Globe and Mail. 1993. Food rots as UN troops focus on military action. Globe and Mail [Toronto], 12 Jul.

——— 1997. The silent debate on foreign policy. Globe and Mail [Toronto], 19 May, p. A18. Editorial.

GOC (Government of Canada). 1982. Canada's relations with Latin America and the Caribbean: final report of the House of Commons Subcommittee on Canada's Relations with Latin America and the Caribbean. GOC, Ottawa, ON, Canada.

——— 1986. Independence and internationalism: report of the Special Joint Committee of the Senate and the House of Commons on Canada's International Relations. GOC, Ottawa, ON, Canada.

——— 1988. Supporting the five: Canada and the Central American peace process: the first report of the House of Commons Special Committee on the Peace Process in Central America. GOC, Ottawa, ON, Canada.

——— 1995a. Canada in the world. GOC, Ottawa, ON, Canada.

——— 1995b. Towards a rapid reaction capability for the United Nations. GOC, Ottawa, ON, Canada.

——— 1996. Canadian Policy Roundtable on peace-building: sustaining post-conflict reconstruction. GOC, Ottawa, ON, Canada. 16 pp.

GON (Government of Nicaragua). 1992. Nicaragua medium-term development strategy 1992–1996. Paper presented at the Consultative Group Meeting, 26 Mar, Washington, DC, USA.

Gordon, N. 1994. Beyond peacekeeping: Somalia, the United Nations and the Canadian experience. *In* Molot, M.A.; von Riekhoff, H., ed., Canada among nations 1994: a part of the peace. Carleton University Press, Ottawa, ON, Canada. pp. 284–300.

Greer, V.L. 1954. State Department policy in regard to the Nicaraguan election of 1924. Hispanic American Historical Review, 34(4), 445–467.

Guerreiro Ramos, A. 1981. The new science of organizations: a reconceptualization of the wealth of nations. University of Toronto Press, Toronto, ON, Canada. 210 pp.

Gurr, T.R. 1994. Peoples against states: ethnopolitical conflict and the changing world system. Canadian Security Intelligence Service, Commentary, No. 50, pp. 2–3.

Henderson, S. 1992/93. Zone of uncertainty: Canada and the security architecture in Asia Pacific. Canadian Foreign Policy (Winter), p. 114.

Hervouët, G. 1988. La réinsertion du Viêt-nam dans le système international. Canadian Institute for International Peace and Security, Ottawa, ON, Canada.

Hiebert, C.D.; Epp, J. 1993. Submission of MCCC to the CCIC Foreign Policy Review: a framework for our common future. Mennonite Central Committee Canada, Ottawa, ON, Canada.

Hoffmann, S. 1995. The crisis of liberal internationalism. Foreign Policy, Spring 1995.

Hutchinson, M.R. 1993. Restoring hope: UN Security Council resolutions for Somalia and an expanded doctrine of humanitarian intervention. Harvard International Law Journal, 34(2), 624–640.

IEN (Instituto de Estudios Nicaraguenses). 1995. La gobernalidad y el acuerdo nacional en Nicaragua. IEN, Managua, Nicaragua.

Ignatieff, M. 1997. Unarmed warriors. The New Yorker, 24 Mar, p. 59.

Jackson, R.H. 1993. Armed humanitarianism. International Journal, 48(4), 579–606.

Jan, A. 1996. Peacebuilding in Somalia. International Peace Academy, New York, NY, USA. IPA Policy Briefing Series. 26 pp.

Jana, Z. 1993. African NGOs: halt military operations in Somalia. Third World Resurgence, 36, 9.

Jennar, R.M. 1995. Chroniques cambodgiennes, 1990–1994 : rapports au Forum International des ONG au Cambodge. Centre européen de recherches sur l'Extrême-Orient, Brussels, Belgium; L'Harmattan, Paris, France. 525 pp.

Job, B.; Langdon, F.L. 1993. Canada and the Pacific. *In* Maule, C.J.: Hampson, F.O., ed., Canada among nations 1993–1994: global jeopardy. Carleton University Press, Ottawa, ON, Canada.

Jonah, J. 1993. Humanitarian intervention. *In* Weiss, T.; Minear, L., ed., Humanitarianism across borders: sustaining civilians in times of war. Lynne Rienner Publishers, Boulder, CO, USA. pp. 69–84.

Kamman, W. 1968. A search for stability: United States diplomacy toward Nicaragua 1925–1933. University of Notre Dame Press, Notre Dame, IN, USA. 263 pp.

Karl, T. 1986. Imposing consent? Electorialism vs. democratization in El Salvador. *In* Drake, P.W.; Silva, E., ed., Elections and democratization in Latin America, 1980–1985. University of California Press, San Diego, CA, USA. pp. 9–36.

Karnes, T.L. 1961. Los fracasos de la unión. Instituto Centroamericano de Administración Pública, Costa Rica.

Kedourie, E. 1966. Nationalism (3rd ed.). Hutchison University Library, London, UK. 151 pp.

Korten, D.C. 1990. Getting to the 21st century: voluntary action and the global agenda. Kumarian Press, West Hartford, CT, USA.

Kunder, J. 1992. Somalia — civil strife. Office of US Foreign Disaster Assistance, US Agency for International Development. Washington, DC, USA. Situation Report No. 7. 30 Jan.

LaFeber, W. 1984. Inevitable revolutions: the United States and Central America. W.W. Norton, New York, NY, USA. 378 pp.

Lanuza, A. 1983. Economía y sociedad en la construcción del estado nacional. *In* Lanuza, A.; Vazquez, J.L.; Barahona, A.; Chamorro, A., ed., Economía y sociedad en la construcción del estado en Nicaragua. Instituto Centroamericano de Administración Pública, San José, Costa Rica. pp. 7–138.

Leaning, J. 1993. When the system doesn't work: Somalia 1992. *In* Cahill, K.M., ed., A framework for survival: health, human rights, and humanitarian assistance in conflicts and disasters. Basic Books; the Council on Foreign Relations, New York, NY, USA. pp. 103–120.

Lechervy, C. 1993. Cambodge : de la paix à la démocratie. Problèmes politiques et sociaux, 716 (Dec).

Lizée, P. 1993. The challenge of conflict resolution in Cambodia. Canadian Defence Quarterly, 23 (Sep), 35–44.

MacDonald, F. 1979. Policy and the foreign relations of Canada. Department of External Affairs, Ottawa, ON, Canada. Statements and Speeches, No. 79/15.

MacKenzie, L. 1994. Paper presented at the IDRC Forum Peacekeeping, Peacemaking and Aid, 6 Apr. International Development Research Centre, Ottawa, ON, Canada.

Mackinlay, J. 1993. Armed relief. *In* Weiss, T.; Minear, L., ed., Humanitarianism across borders: sustaining civilians in times of war. Lynne Rienner Publishers, Boulder, CO, USA; London, UK. pp. 85–96.

Makinda, S.M. 1993. Seeking peace from chaos: humanitarian intervention in Somalia. Lynne Rienner Publishers, Boulder, CO, USA. International Peace Academy Occasional Paper Series. 92 pp.

Marchand, De M. 1990. Rôle du Canada en Asie du Sud-Est durant les années 90. 1 May, Montebello, PQ, Canada. Department of External Affairs, Ottawa, ON, Canada.

Martinez Vega, T.; Ghysels, J. 1995. El combate contra la pobreza: un factor determinante ante el desarrollo. Instituto de Investigadión y Desarrollo–Universidad Centroamericana, Managua, Nicaragua.

Maynes, C.W. 1993. Containing ethnic conflict. Foreign Policy, 90 (Spring), 3–21.

McDougall, B. 1991. Press release. Department of External Affairs, Ottawa, ON, Canada. Press Release No. 237, 23 Oct.

——— 1993. Press release. Department of External Affairs, Ottawa, ON, Canada. Press Release No. 127, 2 Jun.

McKenna, B. 1997. Canada, Japan conspire for peace. Globe and Mail [Toronto], 5 Apr.

Millet, R. 1977. Guardians of the dynasty: a history of the US-created Guardia Nacional and the Samoza family. Orbis Books, Maryknoll, NY, USA.

Millwood, D., ed. 1996. The international response to conflict and genocide: lessons from the Rwanda experience. Steering Committee of the Joint Evaluation of Emergency Assistance to Rwanda. Copenhagen, Denmark.

Moncada, J.M. 1973. Estados Unidos en Nicaragua. Ediciones Nicaraguenses de Cultura General, Managua, Nicaragua. 206 pp.

Moreno, D. 1994. The struggle for peace in Central America. University Press of Florida, Gainesville, FL, USA. 251 pp.

Morison, S.E.; Commager, H.S.; Leuchtenburg, W.E. 1980. The growth of the American republic. 2 vols. Oxford University Press, New York, NY, USA.

North, L., ed. 1990. Between war and peace in Central America: choices for Canada. Between the Lines, Toronto, ON, Canada.

Omaar, R. 1994. Somaliland: one thorn at a time. Current History, May 1994.

Oquist, P. 1992. Sociopolitical dynamics of the 1990 Nicaraguan elections. *In* Castro, V.; Prevost, G., ed., The 1990 elections in Nicaragua and their aftermath. Rowmar & Littlefield, Lanham, MD, USA. pp. 1–40.

Ouellet, A. 1994. Notes for an address by the Honourable Andre Ouellet, Minister of Foreign Affairs, to the 49th General Assembly of the United Nations, 29 Sep, New York, NY, USA. Department of Foreign Affairs and International Trade, Ottawa, ON, Canada.

Pallister, D. 1994. When food relief comes out of a gun barrel. Guardian Weekly, 15 May, p. 7.

Przeworski, A. 1986. Some problems in the study of the transition to democracy. *In* O'Donnell, G.; Schmitter, P.C.; Whitehead, L., ed., Transitions from authoritarian rule: prospects for democracy. Johns Hopkins University Press, Baltimore, MD, USA.

Robinson, W.; MacMichael, D. 1990. Intervention in the Nicaraguan election. Cover Action Information Bulletin No. 33.

Ryan, S. 1990. Ethnic conflict and international relations. Dartmouth Publishing Company, Aldershot, UK.

Sahnoun, M. 1994a. Paper presented at the IDRC Forum Peacekeeping, Peacemaking and Aid, 6 Apr. International Development Research Centre, Ottawa, ON, Canada.

——— 1994b. Somalia: the missed opportunities. United States Institute of Peace, Washington, DC, USA. 89 pp.

Sanderson, J.M. 1994. A review of recent peacekeeping operations. Presentation to Pams XVIII. United Nations, New York, NY, USA.

Sartori, G. 1987. The theory of democracy revisited. Chatham House, Chatham, NJ, USA.

Schmitz, G. 1995. Prevention, humanitarian intervention and disaster relief: current challenges for international emergency response mechanisms to natural and man-made crises and conflicts. Research Branch, Library of Parliament, Ottawa, ON, Canada.

Scrooggs, W.O. 1969. Filibusters and financiers: the story of William Walker and his associates. Russell & Russell, New York, NY, USA.

Selser, G. 1981. Sandino. Monthly Review Press, New York, NY, USA. 250 pp.

——— 1984. Nicaragua: de Walker a Somoza. Mex-Sur Editorial, Mexico City, Mexico. 332 pp.

Selva, C. 1948. Un poco de historia, últimos días de la administración del doctor Roberto sacasa y principios del gobierno del general José Santos Zelaya. Ediciones del Gobierno de Guatemala, Guatemala. 154 pp.

Sharp, M. 1973. Vietnam: participation in the International Control Commission as envisaged by Canada. Department of External Affairs, Ottawa, ON, Canada.

SJCERC (Special Joint Committee on the External Relations of Canada). 1986. Independence and internationalism: report of the Special Joint Committee on the External Relations of Canada. Government of Canada, Ottawa, ON, Canada.

SJCRCFP (Special Joint Committee Reviewing Canadian Foreign Policy). 1994. Canada's foreign policy: principles and priorities for the future. Government of Canada, Ottawa, ON, Canada.

Sklar, H. 1988. Washington's war on Nicaragua. Between the Lines, Toronto, ON, Canada.

Slotkin, R. 1985. The fatal environment: the myth of the frontier in the age of industrialization, 1800–1890. Atheneum, New York, NY, USA.

Solis, F.A.; Martin, P. 1992. The role of Salvadorian NGOs in post-war reconstruction. Development in Practice, 2(2), 103–113.

SSCFA (Standing Senate Committee on Foreign Affairs). 1972. The Pacific area: proceedings of the Standing Senate Committee on Foreign Affairs. Senate of Canada, Ottawa, ON, Canada.

Stackhouse, J. 1993. Linkage of aid to rights found useless. Globe and Mail [Toronto], 5 Jan, p. A7.

Stimson, H.L. 1927. American policy in Nicaragua. Charles Scribner's Sons, New York, NY, USA.

Tinoco, V.H. 1988. Conflicto y paz: el proceso negociador centroamericano. Editorial Mestiza, Mexico City, Mexico.

Torres Rivas, E. 1987. Centroamérica: la democracia posible. Editorial Universitaria Centroamericana, San José, Costa Rica.

UN (United Nations). 1992a. UN Document S/23445, 30 Feb. UN, New York, NY, USA.

——— 1992b. United Nations Security Council Resolution 794 (granting the Secretary-General discretion in the further employment of personnel of the United Nations Operation in Somalia). UN, New York, NY, USA. UN Document S/RES/794, 3 Dec.

——— 1993. United Nations Security Council Resolution 837. UN, New York, NY, USA. UN Document S/RES/837, 6 Jun.

UNRISD (United Nations Research Institute for Social Development). 1994. The challenge of rebuilding war-torn societies. Report on the UNRISD Working Seminar at Cartigny, Geneva, 29 November to 1 December 1994. UNRISD, Geneva, Switzerland. 34 pp.

USDS (United States Department of State). 1932. The United States and Nicaragua: a survey of the relations from 1909 to 1932. USDS, Washington, DC, USA. Latin American Series, No. 6.

Utting, P., ed. 1994. Between hope and insecurity: the social consequences of the Cambodian peace process. United Nations Research Institute for Social Development, Geneva, Switzerland. 229 pp.

Vargas, O.R. 1989. Elecciones en Nicaragua, 1912–1982: análisis socio-político. Dilesa, Managua, Nicaragua. 168 pp.

——— 1990. La revolución que inició el progreso: Nicaragua 1893–1909. Consa, Managua, Nicaragua. 278 pp.

Vazquez, J.L. 1983. Luchas políticas y estado oligárquico. *In* Lanuza, A.; Vazquez, J.L.; Barahona, A.; Chamorro, A., ed., Economía y sociedad en la construcción del estado en Nicaragua. Instituto Centroamericano de Administración Pública, San José, Costa Rica. pp. 139–206.

Watson, J. 1993. Peacekeeping troops often misused. Ottawa Citizen, 20 Jan, p. D7.

Weil, R. 1993. Somalia in perspective: when the saints come marching in. Review of African Political Economy, 57 (Jul), 103–109.

Weiss, T.G. 1993. UN military operations after the Cold War: some conceptual problems. Canadian Defence Quarterly, 23 (Sep), 5–9.

WFP (World Food Programme). 1994. WFP Emergency Telex Report/14, 15 Apr. WFP, Rome, Italy.

Wheelock, J. 1980. Democracia y dictadura. Fondo de Cultura Económica, Mexico City, Mexico.

Whig Standard. 1993. Tough love for the UN: peacekeeping needs overhaul. Whig Standard [Kingston], 5 Oct.

Whitehead, L. 1986. The prospects for a political settlement: most options have been foreclosed. *In* Di Palma, G.; Whitehead, L., ed., The Central American impasse. Croom Helm, London, UK. pp. 218–246.

Will, G. 1993. The election in Cambodia: taking stock of a UN mission. Aussenpolitik, 4, 396.

World Bank. 1997. World development report 1977: the state in a changing world. Oxford University Press, New York, NY, USA. 354 pp.

YCISS (York Centre for International and Strategic Studies). 1986. Central America and peacekeeping: a workshop report. YCISS, Toronto, ON, Canada.

York, G. 1993. Laying a fresh foundation. Globe and Mail [Toronto], 2 Feb, p. A5.

Zartman, I.W. 1985. Ripe for resolution: conflict and intervention in Africa. Oxford University Press, Oxford, UK. 260 pp.

About the Institution

The International Development Research Centre (IDRC) is committed to building a sustainable and equitable world. IDRC funds developing-world researchers, thus enabling the people of the South to find their own solutions to their own problems. IDRC also maintains information networks and forges linkages that allow Canadians and their developing-world partners to benefit equally from a global sharing of knowledge. Through its actions, IDRC is helping others to help themselves.

About the Publisher

IDRC Books publishes research results and scholarly studies on global and regional issues related to sustainable and equitable development. As a specialist in development literature, IDRC Books contributes to the body of knowledge on these issues to further the cause of global understanding and equity. IDRC publications are sold through its head office in Ottawa, Canada, as well as by IDRC's agents and distributors around the world.